YORK NOTES

The Adventures of Huckleberry Finn

Mark Twain

Notes by Sandra Redding

 Longman   York Press

YORK PRESS
322 Old Brompton Road, London SW5 9JH

Pearson Education Limited
Edinburgh Gate, Harlow,
Essex CM20 2JE, United Kingdom
Associated companies, branches and representatives throughout the world

First published 1998
Second impression 1999

ISBN 0–582–36830–8

Designed by Vicki Pacey, Trojan Horse, London
Illustrated by Karen Donnelly
Map by Celia Hart and Karen Donnelly
Phototypeset by Gem Graphics, Trenance, Mawgan Porth, Cornwall
Colour reproduction and film output by Spectrum Colour
Produced by Addison Wesley Longman China Limited, Hong Kong

CONTENTS

PREFACE

York Notes are designed to give you a broader perspective on works of literature studied at GCSE and equivalent levels. We have carried out extensive research into the needs of the modern literature student prior to publishing this new edition. Our research showed that no existing series fully met students' requirements. Rather than present a single authoritative approach, we have provided alternative viewpoints, empowering students to reach their own interpretations of the text. York Notes provide a close examination of the work and include biographical and historical background, summaries, glossaries, analyses of characters, themes, structure and language, cultural connections and literary terms.

If you look at the Contents page you will see the structure for the series. However, there's no need to read from the beginning to the end as you would with a novel, play, poem or short story. Use the Notes in the way that suits you. Our aim is to help you with your understanding of the work, not to dictate how you should learn.

York Notes are written by English teachers and examiners, with an expert knowledge of the subject. They show you how to succeed in coursework and examination assignments, guiding you through the text and offering practical advice. Questions and comments will extend, test and reinforce your knowledge. Attractive colour design and illustrations improve clarity and understanding, making these Notes easy to use and handy for quick reference.

York Notes are ideal for:
- Essay writing
- Exam preparation
- Class discussion

The author of these notes, Sandra Redding, is a Senior Teacher in Leeds, and has considerable experience of teaching at all high school age levels. She is a senior examiner in English and English Literature for a major GCSE examining board.

The text used in these Notes is the Puffin Classics edition, published in 1994.

PART ONE

INTRODUCTION

HOW TO STUDY A NOVEL

You have bought this book because you wanted to study a novel on your own. This may supplement classwork.

- You will need to read the novel several times. Start by reading it quickly for pleasure, then read it slowly and carefully. Further readings will generate new ideas and help you to memorise the details of the story.
- Make careful notes on themes, plot and characters of the novel. The plot will change some of the characters. Who changes?
- The novel may not present events chronologically. Does the novel you are reading begin at the beginning of the story or does it contain flashbacks and a muddled time sequence? Can you think why?
- How is the story told? Is it narrated by one of the characters or by an all-seeing ('omniscient') narrator?
- Does the same person tell the story all the way through? Or do we see the events through the minds and feelings of a number of different people.
- Which characters does the narrator like? Which characters do you like or dislike? Do your sympathies change during the course of the book? Why? When?
- Any piece of writing (including your notes and essays) is the result of thousands of choices. No book had to be written in just one way: the author could have chosen other words, other phrases, other characters, other events. How could the author of your novel have written the story differently? If events were recounted by a minor character how would this change the novel?

Studying on your own requires self-discipline and a carefully thought-out work plan in order to be effective. Good luck.

Mark Twain is the pseudonym of the writer Samuel Langhorne Clemens, born in Florida, Missouri, in 1835.

Early life

Clemens's father was a lawyer, who came originally from Virginia; his mother was born in Kentucky. When he was four, his family moved to Hannibal, Missouri, the true setting for the fictional St Petersburg of the novel *The Adventures of Huckleberry Finn*, where Samuel lived until he was eighteen years old. During this time he met some of the real people whom he used later as models for the characters in his novel.

Close links between his early experiences and the setting for his novel.

When Samuel was twelve years old his father died. The boy began work as a printer's apprentice, working with his older brother Orion who was an editor. As a journeyman printer he later travelled quite widely. He took a steamboat journey down the Mississippi, fell in love with the river and began a career working on the ships sailing the Mississippi.

Clemens was given his licence as a steamboat pilot in 1859. However, the American Civil War, which broke out in 1861, effectively put an end to the freedom to sail the river, and also changed the way of life along its banks. Following the restoration of peace in 1865, more modern systems of travel and transport developed, and the former 'romantic' steamship journey lost importance.

Later employment

He left the Mississippi at the outbreak of the Civil War, and took a number of different jobs which involved travel across the continent. Increasingly, he was turning towards writing as a career, and he adopted the pseudonym Mark Twain about this time. The name, by the way, is a cry used by river boatmen who take soundings to measure the depth of water for safe travel. The cry would be 'by the mark twain' (meaning two fathoms, i.e. twelve feet).

In 1870 Twain married Olivia Langdon, and it is reputed that she affected his writing by offering criticism of his work, which did not always please him. He was certainly often critical of her.

From 1865, when his first book called *Jumping Frog* appeared, Twain published a number of different writings, not all of them novels. You may be familiar with some of the most famous stories, as they are not only enjoyable works of fiction in themselves but also the subject of a number of films and television productions, such as *The Adventures of Tom Sawyer* and *The Prince and the Pauper*.

In later life Twain was involved in a variety of businesses which failed, and he became bankrupt.

In order to make money to pay off his debts he began travelling again. His later writing is marked by bitter cynicism, and there are a number of pieces in which Twain is very critical of world affairs.

Twain died in Redding, Connecticut, in April 1910, at the age of 75.

His influence   Mark Twain is a humorist, but also a social commentator, the best of his work characterised by all of the qualities that we find in *The Adventures of Huckleberry Finn*. Many present-day writers see Twain as introducing a new, original form of the American novel. This is due partly to his choice of an idiomatic style of narration, but partly also to his main theme, the criticism of civilisation and culture in American society.

CONTEXT & SETTING

The novel *The Adventures of Huckleberry Finn* is set in a small town on the Mississippi River, called St Petersburg. This is a fictitious name for the town of

Hannibal, Missouri, where Twain spent much of his childhood.

Twain wanted to write about 'boy-life out on the Mississippi'.

Although the novel was published in 1884 the setting and the contextual background are, as Twain declares himself, 'forty or fifty years ago', that is, before the American Civil War of 1861–5, and at a time when the Mississippi River was an important means of communication.

This setting was also used in his earlier novel *The Adventures of Tom Sawyer*, where it is obvious that Twain was inspired by his childhood memories. However, *The Adventures of Huckleberry Finn* moves away from this happy atmosphere, and is characterised by more emphasis on squalor and hypocrisy (see Themes).

Slavery as a system

In *The Adventures of Huckleberry Finn* Southern society is shown to accept unquestioningly the principle of slavery, the right to own other people as if they were a bought possession, because of the colour of their skin.

'A sound heart and a deformed conscience come into collision' (Twain) on Huck.

The conflict between what is morally right and what is legally enforced, is at the heart of the novel, seen in Huck's internal debates with himself (see Characters and also Themes).

• The system of slavery was a long established part of life in the Americas, fuelled by trade with some countries in Western Europe. Traders in 'black gold' as it was called would travel to the shores of Africa, an undeveloped and largely unexplored country, capture as many black people, men, women and children, as possible, and then transport them to the Southern states of America mainly for sale as workers on the farms and plantations. Southern economy largely depended on agriculture, having little industry at that time, and cotton and tobacco were important crops. Large numbers of workers were needed for these farms. Other black people were used as domestic servants.

- A gulf developed between the Southern and the Northern states, with the South taking offence at the Northern states' denunciation of slavery as immoral. This was one of the reasons for the outbreak of the American Civil War, although there were other more fundamental, political reasons, foremost among them the wish to create a unified country (the United States).

How far does Huck accept these ideas throughout the novel?

- The system which grew up around Southern attitudes to their slaves denied that black people felt human emotions, and maintained that they were a naive and child-like people who would starve without Southern protection. This provided some moral justification for the maintenance of slavery.

Huck's perception

Twain presents this issue of slavery through Huck's eyes, allowing him to represent Southern views and yet to question their morality.

The Mississippi River

The river was a major artery of transport and commun-ication at the time of the novel, connecting large areas of the USA, and was very important as such. Twain's first-hand knowledge of the river came from his employment as pilot on a steamboat. The journey down the Mississippi has a **symbolic** (see Literary Terms) function as well as a physical one, bringing Huck into contact with a variety of people along its shores, and marking the development of his character as he observes their lifestyles.

Which characters does Huck sympathise with, and which does he condemn?

- The wide variety and number of characters in the novel represent the identity of people who inhabited the Southern states. Some are seen more sympathetically as victims of the unscrupulous, but the majority of them are condemned by Twain for living by an outdated code of behaviour, with a misplaced belief in 'honour' (see Themes).

Frontier life

At this time also, there were large areas of land remaining hostile and unsettled. It was a time of the opening up of the continent, with the opportunity to choose land freely and settle it, but frontiersfolk had to be brave, hardy and adventurous.

Huck has all of the qualities of frontier people, brave, wild and free.

- Tom at the end of the novel indicates clearly that the 'Territory' was a largely uncivilised and unsettled area, and that there were adventures to be had amongst the indigenous population of Indians. The loss of this freedom to roam and settle without restriction after the Civil War was one Twain regretted.

Changes in the South

Industrialisation, the replacement of the small settlements by larger groups, the movement from the river as a form of life and transport, all began to occur following the end of the Civil War in 1865.

The cultural divide which had always existed between North and South widened even further, but there was another, deeper division observed by Twain. The North he regarded as notably freer and less restrictive, whereas the South seemed to him slower, more set in its ways. Twain himself noted, on his travels during the 1880s, the difference between the peoples of the South and the North, 'the people [in the North] don't dream, they work'.

Modern application

- Huck as a character distrusts civilisation and its restrictive powers over individuals.
- In the novel Twain presents us with a view of language which can be used by people for their own ends, to manipulate and to cheat.

Both these themes are equally applicable to our time.

PART TWO

SUMMARIES

GENERAL SUMMARY

The story of Huckleberry Finn is told by the title character himself, using his own **dialect** and **idiom** (see Literary Terms).

Chapters 1–4:
Huck's life
with the
Widow
Douglas

Huck summarises his present situation and tells us how in *The Adventures of Tom Sawyer* he and his friend Tom faced robbers and found gold which when shared evenly between them gave them $6000 each. Huck has asked Judge Thatcher to look after his money, and receives a dollar a day from the interest. He tells us of his ongoing struggle to resist 'sivilizing', mainly achieved by escaping to go adventuring with Tom Sawyer. One day Huck sees distinctive boot marks in the snow outside the widow's house, and realises his father is back, looking for him and his money. He forces the Judge to accept his money as a gift to prevent his father from getting it. Huck returns to his room one night, following an adventure with Tom, to find his father waiting for him.

Chapters 5–7:
Huck's father

Huck's father has turned up because he wants Huck's money. He is furious when he realises that the Judge has it, threatening to go to court to force him to give it up. Realising what a bad father Huck has, Widow Douglas and the Judge try to gain custody of the boy in the courts, but are refused. His father is angry at Huck for 'putting on frills and trying to be better than him' (p. 28), so he kidnaps him and takes him to a cabin in the woods where he keeps him locked up. Huck is not unhappy with this life for a time, but then he realises that his father's drunkenness is dangerous and plans to escape. He stages his own death and runs away to Jackson's Island in the middle of the Mississippi River.

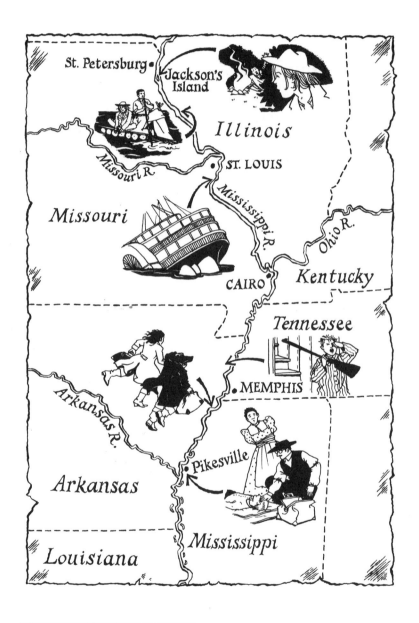

Chapters 8–18: Adventures on the river

On the island he meets Jim, Miss Watson's slave, who has run away after overhearing that she is thinking about selling him. Together Jim and Huck decide to sail down the Mississippi as far as Cairo, then take a steamship passage for the Northern states where Jim can gain his freedom.

'What did that poor old woman do to you, that you could treat her so mean?' (p. 118).

Huck sees the plan as an adventure at first, but increasingly questions the morality of his actions in stealing Jim from Miss Watson. During the course of this journey, Huck and Jim meet a number of different people who live by and on the river. They have many adventures during which Huck witnesses theft, fraud, violence and death. At one point Huck decides to give Jim up to slave catchers, but at the last minute his conscience asserts itself, and his friendship with Jim prevents him. Gradually the fugitives come to realise that they have missed the town of Cairo and are drifting further south. They intend to find a canoe, and sail back up river. However, the raft is run down by a steamship and the two are separated.

Huck swims ashore and is given shelter by the Grangerford family who have a long-standing feud with a neighbouring family, the Shepherdsons. Huck witnesses the final battle between the families, when most of the Grangerfords are killed. Jim has survived the wreck of the raft, and the two are reunited to continue their journey down the river.

Chapters 19–31: Exploitation by the King and the Duke

Two confidence tricksters ask Huck and Jim for help to escape their pursuers. One claims to be the Duke of Bridgewater and the other the King of France. They play a number of tricks on the townspeople they meet, all designed to exploit people's follies and to steal money from them. They put on plays, pretend to be missionaries, and eventually attempt to rob a family by pretending to be brothers of the recently deceased Peter Wilks. Huck becomes directly involved at this point.

He removes the money they have stolen and hides it in Peter Wilks's coffin. The frauds are exposed shortly after this when the real brothers arrive, and Huck escapes to the raft. Unfortunately for him, the two men also escape and return to the raft with Huck and Jim.

After a short journey further down the river, the tricksters, having lost all of their money, sell Jim to a Mr Phelps, whom Huck discovers to be the husband of Tom Sawyer's Aunt Sally. Huck feels responsible for Jim and remembers their friendship on the raft. Despite his conflicting ideas about the rights and wrongs of slavery he determines to help Jim to escape.

Chapters 32–43: Jim's 'escape' and Huck's future

Huck meets Aunt Sally and is mistaken for Tom Sawyer, her nephew, whose visit she is expecting. Tom arrives and pretends to be his own brother Sid. Together they plan the escape of Jim, with Tom forming a plan which follows the **Romantic** (see Literary Terms) tradition in fiction. The two boys, Tom out of enjoyment, but Huck reluctantly, formulate an increasingly complex plan to rescue Jim and eventually succeed. Unfortunately, during Jim's escape Tom is shot and Huck has to fetch a doctor to help him.

Because of this Tom and Jim are both discovered in hiding and returned to the Phelps farm, and the boys' true identities are revealed. Aunt Polly arrives to claim the boys, and it is discovered that Miss Watson gave Jim his freedom before her recent death, which Tom had known about. Huck is told that his own father is dead, his body seen by Jim in the floating house at the start of their journey months before. The three characters arrange to run away into the Territory and have adventures among the Indians. Huck declares that he will probably go before the others as he is about to be adopted by Aunt Sally, who will also try to 'sivilize' him.

DETAILED SUMMARIES

CHAPTERS 1–4: HUCK'S LIFE WITH THE WIDOW DOUGLAS

CHAPTER 1

Huckleberry Finn introduces himself and explains his circumstances. We are told of his past adventures with Tom Sawyer, that they found robbers' gold and shared the money between them. Huck, although rich now, thinks that his allowance of a dollar a day is 'more than a body could tell what to do with' (p. 1). He has been given a home by the Widow Douglas and her sister Miss Watson, and tells us of their attempts to civilise him, to educate him and teach him about religion.

We become aware, through Huck's simple and humorous way of looking at life, of his essential loneliness and his yearning to lead the less restricted life of nature. He hears a cat's cry outside and leaves through the window to meet Tom Sawyer.

COMMENT

This opening chapter provides the reader with the information necessary for understanding how the novel will work: character, themes and plot are all given to us.

We are introduced to the characteristics, attitudes and beliefs that make up Huck. Huck is seen as a simple, uncomplicated boy with homespun superstitious beliefs, shown in his reaction to killing a spider.

How does the style of telling the story help you to understand it?

Mark Twain allows his main character, Huckleberry Finn, to tell the story directly to us in the idiom of the Southern states of America. The first word 'you' indicates that Huck is taking the direct approach, telling his version of events in the first person (see Language & Style). This indicates how important the *method* of presentation is, as well as the *substance* of the story.

The first paragraph, referring to the book previously written, *The Adventures of Tom Sawyer*, makes it clear that Huck is addressing an audience. It is possible to hear the voice of the author here, in talking about 'truth' within books. This, coupled with the closing paragraph of the novel (p. 386) which refers to the 'trouble' of writing a book, presents the voice of the author who explored many of his own difficulties with Southern life in this novel (see Context & Setting).

'A mostly true book; with some stretchers' (p. 1). Are there different 'types' of truth?

Truth is one of the themes explored in the novel, and Huck's interpretation of it is important. He accepts that people do not always tell the truth, but does not moralise about this.

In the novel Huck himself frequently fabricates identities and stories for himself to explain his actions. But Twain draws distinctions between essential and non-essential truths, between lying for gain and 'story telling' (see Themes).

There is a clear sense of the restrictions imposed on him in Huck's description of his present circumstances. He uses the humour of describing 'civilised' food to indicate how unsettling his life is for him. It is separate and organised, rather than, like life, 'in a barrel of odds and ends ... mixed up' with the effect that 'things go better' (p. 2).

Huck's honest and forthright approach to life immediately endears him to us, and allows us insight into his mind and feelings. These things are important so that, as we share his adventures, and are asked to examine his conscience alongside him, we can fully understand the struggle that goes on within him as to 'right' and 'wrong'.

GLOSSARY

stretchers exaggerations of the truth

Moses and the Bulrushers a bible story in the Book of Exodus , which tells how Moses, the eventual leader of the Israelites, chosen by God, is found as a baby floating on the Nile among bulrushes, and reared by the Egyptian princess niggers accepted Southern term for Negroes. Modern white attitudes find the term insulting, but it is suggestive of the status of black slaves at the time of writing, and is used constantly throughout the novel

CHAPTER 2

Tom and Huck escape to have an adventure. Huck trips up as they pass Jim's cabin (Jim is a slave owned by Miss Watson) and they have to sit perfectly still to avoid discovery. Tom decides to play a trick on Jim which results in Jim believing he is bewitched. They meet the rest of their gang and agree to form a Band of Robbers with bloodthirsty rules. They discuss how they will ransom kidnapped people, but do not understand what 'ransom' means. They agree to start their life of crime as soon as possible, and Huck returns home with his clothes dirty and muddy.

COMMENT

Observe how description is used here to involve the reader in the story.

The lengthy and very funny description at the start of this chapter about Huck's need to scratch an itch and the growing impossibility of resisting the urge (pp. 6–7) allows Huck to describe an experience vividly.

The dependence on superstition as a part of life is explored quite thoroughly, with comic references to witchcraft and spell casting. Jim is shown to be a kindred spirit to Huck, equally superstitious.

Huck's night-time life of adventure is seen as a direct contrast to his daytime civilised life.

There is comedy and a **Romantic** (see Literary Terms) approach to adventure underlying the boys' attitude to kidnapping. This is found again in the spirit of the later chapters of the novel when Tom and Huck attempt to free the imprisoned Jim from captivity (Chapters 34–9).

Compare and contrast Tom and Huck in these early chapters.

There are significant differences between the characters of Tom and Huck as drawn here. Huck emerges as a practical thinker and not such a child of the imagination as Tom. Tom enjoys contriving adventures which are complex and full of fun. However, their general innocence and simple view of life are emphasised by the rules of their gang and their approach to the life of crime they intend to pursue.

GLOSSARY   **tanyard** a place where leather was made
skiff a small, light rowing boat

CHAPTER 3   Huck is encouraged by Miss Watson to pray, but he does not believe it is of any use. He is told that his father is presumed drowned, but does not believe that either, 'I judged that the old man would turn up again by-and-by, though I wished he wouldn't' (p. 16).

The Band of Robbers have some adventures, mainly dictated by Tom the **Romantic**, but Huck eventually resigns after an attack on rich 'Spanish merchants' and 'A-rabs', which is nothing more than disturbing a Sunday school picnic. Tom tries to pretend that the attack was spoiled because genies intervened, but Huck rationalises this as another of Tom's stories.

COMMENT   Religion is seen as a restrictive influence on Huck. He is told he should pray but cannot believe in it; his practical approach to life sees no 'advantage' (p. 15) in it.

How are we encouraged to be more sympathetic to Huck in this chapter?   He also thinks in a practical fashion about the possibility that his father is dead. Huck relies upon himself and his own powers and judgement. He is mentally different from Tom, not only unable to share fully in the imaginative play the Band indulges in, but also unable to see any enjoyment in it. Huck is being depicted as an isolated and yet a self-sufficient character.

GLOSSARY   **fat up** put on weight
ornery ordinary, unremarkable
hived robbed
primer-class youngest class, primary class at school

Don Quixote a satirical romance by Miguel de Cervantes, published in 1605, whose hero has a number of fantastic and absurd adventures. It is typical of Tom's character that he would enjoy and wish to imitate such adventures

CHAPTER 4

Huck seems to be settling more easily into his civilised life. He accepts school and the demands made on him by the Widow Douglas, 'I liked the old ways best, but I was getting so I liked the new ones too' (p. 20).

During the winter he recognises his father's distinctive heel prints in the snow outside the Widow Douglas's house. He immediately rushes to give the rest of his money to Judge Thatcher to prevent his father from getting it, and consults Jim about his fortune to see what the future will hold. He returns to his room to find his father waiting for him.

COMMENT

This chapter is a starting point for exploring the tension between Huck's inner self and his outward conformity. His struggles to accept his new life produce an uneasy peace, but he manages to tolerate them. He accepts his present circumstances, not going beyond the here and now.

Superstition takes the place of organised religion in his life. He is concerned particularly about bad luck, and on discovering that his father has returned, consults Jim's lucky charm. What Jim tells him is amusing, yet fatalistic, with Jim asserting that Huck is 'gwyne to git hung' and that he should avoid water (p. 24), which is ironic as the novel is about adventures on the Mississippi River.

We grow closer to Jim here, and recognise the similarities of views between him and Huck. Both are fatalistic, but not pessimistic. Everything that happens to them is part of life.

GLOSSARY

played hookey truanted from school

Identify the speaker.

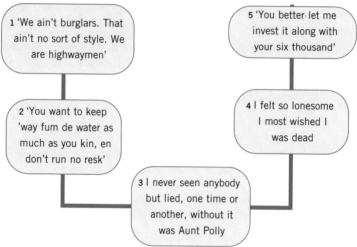

1 'We ain't burglars. That ain't no sort of style. We are highwaymen'

5 'You better let me invest it along with your six thousand'

2 'You want to keep 'way fum de water as much as you kin, en don't run no resk'

4 I felt so lonesome I most wished I was dead

3 I never seen anybody but lied, one time or another, without it was Aunt Polly

Identify the person 'to whom' this comment refers.

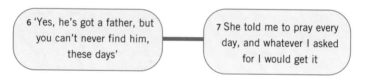

6 'Yes, he's got a father, but you can't never find him, these days'

7 She told me to pray every day, and whatever I asked for I would get it

Check your answers on page 95.

 ## B *Consider these issues.*

a The style Twain uses in presenting the story to us, and how it makes the story more believable.

b The character and personality of Huck himself, and how Twain makes us sympathise with him.

c How Twain uses description to hold his readers' attention.

CHAPTERS 5–7: HUCKS'S FATHER

CHAPTER 5

Huck is surprised and a little frightened at first to see his shiftless father. Old Finn has heard about Huck's fortune, and has come to demand it. He refuses to accept that Judge Thatcher will not release it. He complains about his son's 'frills' (p. 26) and demands that he leave school. He takes what money Huck has and gets drunk. Widow Douglas and Judge Thatcher try to gain legal custody of Huck but a new judge refuses, saying that families should not be separated. He attempts to reform Huck's father and takes him into his own house. However, after finding him drunk again, the judge realises he has been made a fool of.

COMMENT

Huck's father is shown to be a worthless drunk, only interested in selfish gain.

Think about how Twain develops the idea that Huck can only rely on himself.

The vivid physical description which opens the chapter builds up a clear picture of a ragged, dirty and uncaring man, and turns the reader's sympathy unreservedly towards Huck.

Huck's account of the legal wrangle for his custody is dispassionate. The objective description of his father's actions provides a powerful insight into the life that Huck would have with him, much more effectively presented than if Huck were angry or frightened. Huck's isolation, emotionally and physically, from society is highlighted. He will have to protect himself.

GLOSSARY

slouch broad-brimmed soft hat
General Washington George Washington, first President of the United States (1732–99)
bullyragged swore at
temperance abstinence from alcohol
pledge a formal promise to avoid alcohol
forty-rod raw whisky

CHAPTERS 6–7

Huck's father applies to court to get the control of Huck's money away from Judge Thatcher. While waiting he regularly becomes drunk and creates a disturbance. Widow Douglas threatens to make trouble for him, so he kidnaps Huck, taking him deep into the woods to his log cabin.

Think about Huck's reaction to his new lifestyle and why he is happy at first.

Huck easily settles into enjoying this life, with its freedom from rules, but eventually realises that his father is dangerous, likely to leave him locked in with no chance of escape. His father tells him of a further attempt by the widow to adopt him, and Huck considers escaping from them all. One dreadful night, Huck's father becomes so drunk that he imagines Huck is the Angel of Death, and threatens to kill him. Huck, frightened, spends the night with a loaded gun on his knees.

The next day Huck makes plans to escape.

Look at Huck's quick-witted actions and how he manages his escape.

His father leaves the cabin locking Huck in. Huck breaks out and takes all of the food and equipment with him. He kills a wild pig and stages his own death, making it look as though the cabin had been attacked by robbers and he had been killed and dragged off to the river. He then sails off down the river towards Jackson's Island.

COMMENT

These chapters provide a realistic reason for Huck's defection from society: on one side there is the free but dangerous life he lives with his father; on the other the restricted life of civilisation with the widow. Huck's escape can therefore be seen less as a simple escape from circumstances, and more as a deliberate attempt to leave behind the life that has been forced upon him.

The bitter criticism of Huck's father about the 'govment' (pp. 35–6) begins humorously with his

The law will not protect Huck from his father.

comments about the unfairness of a law which prevents him from claiming his rights: the right to bring up his son as he wishes; the right to claim financial help from his son when he is old enough to work; the right to use his son's money as his own. The **irony** (see Literary Terms) of his comments is not lost on the reader who sees him in his true colours as worthless and selfish.

This ironic tone becomes more savage when old Finn discusses the rights of a 'free nigger' to vote.

How is Southern society presented here?

Twain incisively forces the reader to become involved in the slavery debate, by his use of contrasts. Huck's father meets and describes a seemingly respectable negro as 'a prowling, thieving, infernal, white-shirted free nigger' (p. 37): as a white man, of whatever character, old Finn is regarded as superior in Southern society's eyes. This discussion lays the foundation for the later battle in Huck's conscience, between what society expects of him and what his good sense and emotions tell him about Jim.

Huck is shown to be a resourceful young boy, unwilling to accept a way of life he dislikes, and revelling in the freedom of lifestyle in the woods. His resourcefulness is to be tested on numerous occasions throughout the novel.

GLOSSARY

Chapter 6

tow rough flax or hemp

mulatter mulatto, a term for the child of a negro and a white person

nabob minor Indian prince

Angel of Death Bible story from Exodus; the last plague in Egypt, sent by God to force the Pharaoh to release the Israelites, was the killing in one night of the first-born sons of all Egyptian families, by the Angel of Death

Chapter 7

'trot' line long line of fishing hooks fixed to a river bank

A *Identify the speaker.*

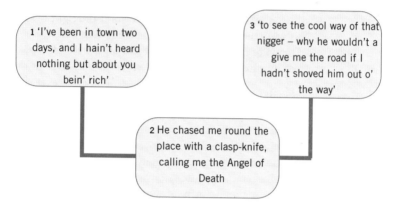

1 'I've been in town two days, and I hain't heard nothing but about you bein' rich'

3 'to see the cool way of that nigger – why he wouldn't a give me the road if I hadn't shoved him out o' the way'

2 He chased me round the place with a clasp-knife, calling me the Angel of Death

Identify the person 'to whom' this comment refers.

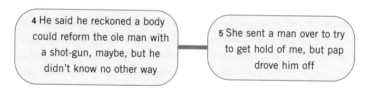

4 He said he reckoned a body could reform the ole man with a shot-gun, maybe, but he didn't know no other way

5 She sent a man over to try to get hold of me, but pap drove him off

Check your answers on page 95.

 B *Consider these issues.*

a How Twain shows us Huck's isolation and essential loneliness.

b How far we understand Huck by the end of these chapters.

c How the style of story-telling, with the mixture of humour and seriousness, contributes to our enjoyment of the story and understanding of its message.

CHAPTERS 8–18: ADVENTURES ON THE RIVER

CHAPTER 8

After three days in hiding Huck explores the island and finds evidence of a recent fire. At first he retreats into hiding to watch, but then decides to find out what is happening. At night he creeps up to the camp fire and finds Jim.

How are the two characters seen as similar while on the island?

Huck and Jim compare stories, and Huck learns that Jim has run away after hearing that Miss Watson was considering selling him for $800. He is cheerfully confident that there is good fortune in store for him.

COMMENT

This chapter begins the central part of the narrative, the adventures of Huck and Jim as they journey down the Mississippi.

Huck's meeting with Jim widens the perspective of the narrative.

'People would call me a low-down Ablitionist and despise me for keepin mum' (p. 57).

Huck is conscious of the clash between society's expectations and his friendship with Jim when he realises that Jim is a runaway slave, but he chooses to side with Jim. This decision will make a significant impact on Huck's thoughts and cause internal conflict as they journey down the river.

Jim's speech is yet another form of Southern dialect. His language is uncultured, but nevertheless expressive, especially so when he is describing his own superstitions and his experiences. The simplicity of his attitude to money will be evident to the reader in the conflict with the King and Duke later in the novel (Chapters 19–31). Jim's final comment in this chapter, 'I owns myself, en I's wuth eight hund'd dollars' (p. 63) is ironic. The reason he is in hiding is because he does not own himself.

Both characters are fugitives, escaping a society where the rules prevent them from truly 'owning themselves'.

ADVENTURES ON THE RIVER

GLOSSARY
cornpone rough bread

haggled cut

gapped yawned

Ablitionist an Abolitionist – a person working towards emancipation of black slaves. Active in the South up to the Civil War, and despised by most Southern people

sell me down to Orleans as Jim's owner, Miss Watson can sell him. Orleans is further south than Hannibal where Jim currently lives. The further south they lived, the more committed to the system slave owners were

shin out avoid work, run away from work

CHAPTERS 9–10

Jim insists that the two find somewhere safer on the island because the rains are coming.

Look at the power of the descriptions of nature and the weather.

The rains continue for many days and the river rises to cover large parts of the island. One night they rescue a substantial raft which is floating past, and another time they see a frame-built wooden house floating by, uprooted by the storm. On investigating the house they discover the dead body of a man who has been shot. Jim examines the body while Huck removes everything from the house which might be of use to them, including some women's clothes.

Later that week, following a joke played by Huck, Jim is bitten by a rattlesnake. He is ill for four days before he gets better. Huck becomes restless and decides to return to shore to see what is happening. To disguise himself, he wears the female clothes they salvaged from the floating house. He reaches the shore and tries to find out what is happening in town.

COMMENT

These two chapters establish a relationship between Huck and Jim. They share a similar outlook on life and a respect for nature.

The description of the storm is powerful and vivid. There is a glorying in the power of nature here, 'I wouldn't want to be nowhere else but here' (pp. 65–6).

At the end of the novel Jim reveals that the dead man in the house was old Finn (Chapter 43). He has waited for the right opportunity to tell Huck.

GLOSSARY

Chapter 9
reticule lady's small netted handbag

Chapter 10
ha'nting haunting
peart confident

CHAPTER 11

Huck talks to Mrs Judith Loftus.

He learns that his murder has been easily accepted as fact with suspicion falling mainly on his father but also on Jim. Mrs Loftus reports seeing smoke on Jackson's Island and suspects that Jim may be hiding there. Her husband has gone to hire a boat and collect an armed companion, intending to search the island. Mrs Loftus realises that Huck is in disguise. He invents another story for her which she believes, and then quickly leaves to warn Jim. They pull the raft from its hiding place, and set off down the river.

What comic effect is created by Huck's disguise?

COMMENT

The close of this chapter signals the end of the relative tranquillity of Huck's and Jim's stay on the island. They are now two fugitives. Huck is anxious to prevent Jim's capture and acts instinctively to protect his friend from injustice.

The motif of money appears again in this chapter, with Mrs Loftus keen to claim the $300 reward for Jim's capture. The reader by now already understands that to sell Jim for money is morally wrong.

*Is this real
deception, or
forgivable
innocent tale-
telling?*

Huck tells the first of the many tall stories he uses in the text to hide his identity and explain awkward circumstances.

He is a ready and witty story-teller, but not practised enough to maintain his 'lies'. For example he forgets the name he has given and has to construct a new identity.

CHAPTER 12

The two fugitives sail down the Mississippi River until dawn, when they tie up to rest for the day. As night falls again they make formal preparations for a long journey; Jim builds a wigwam to sleep in and to protect their belongings.

*Imagine what
they might see and
feel on this part of
their journey.*

They sail smoothly for many nights. They pass St Louis, having developed a simple nightly routine of Huck buying small provisions, or stealing a chicken or a watermelon. 'Take it all around, we lived pretty high' (p. 88).

They come upon a wrecked steamship which they explore, but on seeing a light they decide to leave quickly to avoid being discovered. Huck overhears two men planning to kill their third companion because he has betrayed them. The third man is tied up and begging for his life. Huck intends to escape in the lifeboat and send for the sheriff. However, Jim tells him that their own raft has broken loose and that they have no means of leaving the wreck.

COMMENT   This chapter fulfils our expected ideas of boyhood adventures, particularly where the heroes are in danger. Tension is created with the discovery of the robbers and their threats to kill their companion.

Think about the growing distinctions being made between Huck's honest morality and the rest of society.

There are clear reminders of Twain's early life as a steamship guide in this chapter. He displays his specific and confident knowledge of the river and steamships.

There is a further glimpse of the simple morality which dominates Huck's life in the humorous discussion of the difference between ' borrowing' and 'stealing'. This childlike exploration of morality endears him to us.

GLOSSARY   **crawfished** crawled on hands and knees
                     treed discovered

CHAPTER 13

Jim and Huck search for a means of escape from the wreck. They find a small lifeboat but the robbers are already loading it. However, when they remember that their companion still has his share of the gold and return to collect it, Huck and Jim steal the boat.

'There ain't no telling but I might come to be a murderer myself' (p. 97).

When they have recovered their own raft, and loaded their new booty, Huck decides to find help for the trapped men. He approaches a village and persuades the ferry-man to set out for the steamship. The river rises again, and Huck sees the wreck rush by. He can do nothing about it.

COMMENT   Huck's bravery and his sensitivity to others' plight are shown here. Despite the fact that both he and Jim are very frightened, they scout the steamship and find, then steal, the boat. Huck's sympathy with the robbers shows us his closeness to humanity as a whole, despite what they have done.

Look for and note further examples of this as the novel progresses.   He notes that the Widow Douglas would be proud of him, a comment which indicates his constant awareness of being an outcast, needing acceptance: ' I wished the widow knowed about it' (p. 101).

This sympathetic understanding also shows the sensitive side to his nature which will develop as he becomes increasingly able to see the humanity in Jim, the slave, even though society demands a different attitude.

GLOSSARY   **spondulicks** wealth

Walter Scott the steamboat is called after the Scottish writer (1771–1832). Twain is again pointing at **Romantic** fiction through this name as Sir Walter Scott was a favourite in the romantic South

trading scow flat-bottomed boat

beatenest best, beating everything else

CHAPTER 14

Huck reads some of the books they have rescued from the steamship and tells Jim about some of the kings he knows about. They discuss the biblical story of Solomon. Jim cannot understand the reason for Solomon's decision. Neither can he understand the need for other languages.

COMMENT   Following the tension of the previous chapter, Twain provides here an amusing interlude as a plot device which allows for further building of relationships and drawing together of the similarities in Huck and Jim.

Consider this as applied to Huck's society as a whole.

They reflect on wealth, and on how rich they are with the booty from the wreck.

The discussion about Solomon is a humorous one, but without any sneering or cynicism on the part of the author. Childish innocence and understanding are maintained here, and the reader enjoys such an uncomplicated attitude to life. Huck's inbuilt Southern attitude to slavery is still obvious. He accepts a limit in the negro's intellectual capacity, 'you can't learn a nigger to argue' (p. 107).

GLOSSARY   **King Sollermun** the bible story used here tells how Solomon, a wise and kindly king of Israel, had to decide who was the rightful mother of a child. He ordered that the child be cut in half so each claimant could have one half. The real mother gave the child to her rival rather than see it killed (Kings 1:3)
Louis Sixteenth King of France, executed by the people in the French Revolution
dolphin dauphin, the official title of the heir to the French throne
Polly-voo-franzy parlez-vous français, translated as 'do you speak French?'

CHAPTER 15

Huck and Jim pursue their plan to sail to Cairo and from there take a steamship for the Northern states and Jim's freedom. In the course of the night fog comes down and Huck in the canoe loses both the raft and Jim. Eventually he regains the raft and finds Jim asleep, exhausted after what had obviously been a rough time.

What do you feel about Huck's trick and Jim's response?

Huck pretends to be asleep and tries to fool Jim into believing that he has dreamed the events. Jim realises he has been fooled. He is hurt and upset that Huck played such a trick when he himself was so worried that

Huck was dead. Huck feels ashamed of himself, and eventually goes to apologise to Jim.

COMMENT   This chapter marks a significant change in the relationship between Jim and Huck, with Jim deeply wounded by Huck's joke, 'trash is what people is dat puts dirt on de head er dey fren's en makes 'em ashamed' (p. 115).

Consider how much Huck has learnt here.

Huck realises how much he wants Jim's friendship and is forced to go against social convention, to 'humble [himself] to a nigger' (p. 115) and see Jim as a human being with feelings: 'I wouldn't done that one if I'd a knowed it would make him feel that way' (p. 115).

This struggle is never fully resolved. Huck is essentially a Southerner, and the rest of the novel increasingly pushes this conflict within him into prominence.

GLOSSARY   **Ohio** a river which joins the Mississippi, flowing down from free states

free States Northern states where there was no slavery

CHAPTER 16

As they drift further south, Jim becomes increasingly nervous about missing the town of Cairo. Huck grows more concerned about the enormity of what he is doing in helping a slave to escape. Huck sees a town and sets off to find out where they are.

What is the consequence to Huck of his actions?

He meets slave catchers looking for five escaped negroes. Huck almost gives Jim up, but instead pretends his family is ill with smallpox. The men give him two twenty dollar pieces and advise him to move on.

Huck and Jim soon realise they have missed Cairo, and after losing the canoe (which they need for the upstream journey on the Ohio) they are forced to sail on down the Mississippi until they can find another. A steamship passing by overturns the raft. Huck loses Jim and swims for the shore.

COMMENT When Jim becomes more open about his plans and hopes for the future, Huck increasingly feels uncomfortable.

'What did that poor old woman ever do to you, that you could treat her so mean?' (p. 118).

We are confronted with the dilemma of Huck, a good-hearted boy, genuinely believing in the right of one human being to own another, but feeling confusion because of the friendship he feels for Jim.

Jim's friendship for Huck, and his simple-hearted trust ('de on'y white genlman dat ever kep' his promise to ole Jim' (p. 119)) draw the reader into Huck's dilemma.

Twain creates another adventurous episode with the tense and vivid description of the ramming by the steamship. This dramatic event marks a temporary return to a boys' adventure story.

At this point Twain stopped writing the novel he had begun immediately after completing *The Adventures of Tom Sawyer*. He was to struggle to complete it over the next seven years.

CHAPTERS 17–18

Huck is given shelter by the Grangerfords, presented as a typical Southern family. The family has a long-standing feud with the neighbouring Shepherdsons, but the youngest Grangerford boy, Buck, does not know what started the feud. Following the church service on Sunday, Huck is asked to return to church to collect Miss Sophia Grangerford's bible, and finds a note inside it. He then discovers that Jim and the raft have survived intact. Huck returns to the house to find that

Miss Sophia has run away with Harney Shepherdson, and the whole Grangerford family has turned out to get her back. Huck witnesses the final battle in which the Grangerford family are wiped out, including Buck. Sickened, he returns to the raft.

COMMENT

These two chapters detail some of Twain's bitterness with Southern life, given voice in Huck's astute observations on behaviour and tradition.

Look for the changes in tone in these chapters: serious, humorous, angry, etc.

He describes the clutter of household ornaments, unconsciously holding up to ridicule the appalling poetry, 'she would slap down a line' (p. 138), and dreadful art, 'she was crying into a handkerchief and had a dead bird laying on its back in its other hand with its heels up' (p. 135). Huck's down-to-earth attitude provides several amusing comments on the Grangerford lifestyle.

Ironical comments on the Southern code.

Much is made of the Grangerfords' courteous manners. The **irony** (see Literary Terms) becomes more strident in the description of the church service where a sermon on brotherly love is admired despite the violent feud, and the final killing of the Grangerford men (see Language & Style, and also Themes).

Huck's final response, 'It made me so sick I most fell out of the tree' (p. 153) aptly expresses the reader's own feelings.

The two fugitives return gladly to the simple life of the raft: 'there warn't no home like a raft … you feel mighty free and easy and comfortable on a raft' (p. 155).

GLOSSARY   *Chapter 17*
Pilgrim's Progress, Friendship's Offering, Henry Clay, Washingtons and Lafayettes a range of typical works of literature and historical paintings and portraits that could be found in a Southern parlour. They were chosen by Twain as typical of the Southern lifestyle

Chapter 18
Prefore-ordestination two words confused, predestination and foreordination, both expressing the belief that one's fate is determined before birth

A Identify the speaker.

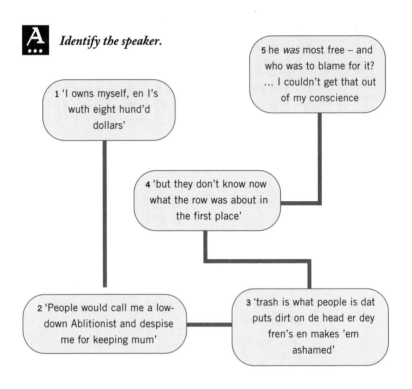

5 he *was* most free – and who was to blame for it? ... I couldn't get that out of my conscience

1 'I owns myself, en I's wuth eight hund'd dollars'

4 'but they don't know now what the row was about in the first place'

2 'People would call me a low-down Ablitionist and despise me for keeping mum'

3 'trash is what people is dat puts dirt on de head er dey fren's en makes 'em ashamed'

Check your answers on page 95.

B Consider these issues.

a How Twain presents Huck's gradual exploration of his conscience with regard to Jim and slavery.

b The different types of people met so far and Huck's response to them.

c The structure of the story – the points of high tension and the intervals of calm.

d How the river is presented to us as almost a character in its own right.

CHAPTERS 19–31: EXPLOITATION BY THE KING AND THE DUKE

CHAPTER 19

A peaceful chapter with a lengthy description of Huck and Jim sailing calmly down the river. The tranquillity of the journey is broken by the arrival of two men, escaping capture.

Huck knows they are both false, but decides to keep quiet.

They join Huck and Jim, and tell them about themselves. One of the men announces himself to be the rightful Duke of Bridgewater from England, and the other, not to be outdone, declares that he is a king, the heir to the throne of France.

COMMENT

The beginning of this chapter is in direct contrast to the pace of the previous events, as if Twain is providing a healing space for Huck and Jim on the river. There is a beautiful and peaceful description of life upon the river in general, reminiscent of Twain's own experiences as a steamship pilot (see Context & Setting, and Language & Style). The harmony is abruptly broken by the arrival of two men.

Consider the discordant effect of such men on life on the raft.

Huck's detailed description helps us to visualise the men. Their conversation is reported in full. The ironic undertone introduced by Huck as they claim their heritage allows us to watch with amusement their attempts to outdo one another.

Huck restates his own adaptability and his unwillingness to cause problems. 'If I never learnt nothing else out of pap, I learnt that the best way to get along with his kind of people is to let them have their own way' (p. 166). By the end of the chapter the reader has become aware of the intrusion and threat brought aboard by the men.

Exploitation by the king and the duke

GLOSSARY   **galluses** a form of braces used to hold up trousers
Charlemagne a famous emperor of the Roman Empire which stretched over most of the Western world (742–814)

CHAPTER *20*

Huck makes up an explanation for why he and Jim are on the river, and why they move only at night. The Duke declares that he will find a way for them to travel by day. The two men rehearse scenes from Shakespeare's plays, intending to put on shows for money. They reach the small town of Pokesville, and go ashore. The King addresses the crowd at a camp meeting, pretending to be a reformed pirate needing funds so he can return as a missionary to 'save' other pirates. He collects $87.75 for his work. The Duke sells advertising space and produces a handbill proclaiming Jim a runaway slave with a reward of $200. He declares that this will allow them to move freely down river by day, if they tie Jim up when they see anybody coming.

COMMENT   Beginning with this chapter Huck increasingly becomes critical of the two frauds and the tricks they work on the Southern people as they make their way down river.

Observe Huck's honesty as opposed to the frauds' trickery.   The lives of Huck and Jim have suddenly become much more complicated with the advent of these two men; they are now embroiled in complex confidence tricks. Jim is now treated as a slave on the raft for the first time, when he is to be tied up during the daytime.

Trace the growing closeness of Jim and Huck, in spite of the cultural divide.   From the opening of the chapter the King and Duke abuse Huck's and Jim's generosity; they steal their beds and assume that the fugitives will stand watch while they sleep.

The effect of their presence is to pull Huck further away from his cultural allegiance with white people, and push him closer to Jim in friendship. The child-like simple humour of the two friends contrasts sharply with the cunning deceptions of the two men.

Twain's cynicism about Southern religion.

The ease with which the King works the crowd at the camp meeting emphasises Twain's already cynical attitude towards Southern people; their acceptance of the language of religion without understanding its meaning; their naivety in taking at face value a man's story because it is powerfully told. The story the King tells is decidedly unbelievable, and yet the people's gullibility is complete. There is no sympathy in Twain's description of the willingness of the Southern people to be deceived.

The reward poster for Jim provides another dimension. The two frauds discuss him without reference to his feelings and in this Huck concurs. The reader begins to make his own extended judgements about the treatment of Jim within Southern society, where such a plan, involving the tying up of a man for convenience, can be seen as acceptable.

GLOSSARY   **deck passage** travel on a steamship was variously priced. Deck passage was the cheapest form, offering no cabin accommodation
phrenology a 'scientific' study of personality made by studying bumps on the head

CHAPTER 21

The King and Duke practise their Shakespearean show but have no understanding of the plays themselves. The two men go ashore at Bricksville and put up their handbills advertising the show. At noon Huck witnesses a drunken challenge issued by a man called Boggs to a Colonel Sherburn. Huck sees Boggs killed. The crowd is shocked, and moves to confront the Colonel with the intention of lynching him.

EXPLOITATION BY THE KING AND THE DUKE

COMMENT This chapter is an odd **juxtaposition** (see Literary Terms) of humour and violence.

Language and its oratorical value appear more important than its meaning.

The opening scenes of Shakespeare and the soliloquy that the Duke presents are a mixture of speeches from *Hamlet* and *Macbeth*, making little sense but sounding very grand.

The power of language here is noted by the ingenuous Huck, 'it was perfectly lovely the way he would rip and tear and rair up behind when he was getting it off' (p. 182).

The description of the town itself is vivid and powerful; it is a run-down, neglected place, not only its buildings but also the people are impoverished.

What do the conversations on pages 184–5 tell you about the town?

The town itself is derelict, full of mud, dogs, and the people's behaviour is cruel and senseless. Twain masterfully describes the incident between Boggs and Sherburn, beginning in humour and ending in violence: the humour of the harmless man challenging the Colonel; the agony of the man's daughter; and then the final cold-blooded killing.

'Well, by-and-by somebody said Sherburn ought to be lynched' (p. 191).

Twain's anger with the crowd which acts as a catalyst by encouraging Boggs in laughing at him, then supposedly coaxing him to stop, is clearly evident in the tone of the passage. The response of the crowd to Boggs's death is not immediate. It is the same lazy, laid-back, uncaring attitude that they have displayed all their lives.

GLOSSARY **Capet** an ironic reference by the Duke to the family name of the French monarchy

soliloquy a speech by one actor alone

sick him an instruction to a dog to attack

CHAPTER *22*

The crowd, incensed, has proceeded to the Colonel's house. Sherburn faces them, and insults their manhood and their intentions.

The circus and the frauds' show: a contrast.

The crowd disperses immediately and Huck moves away, and goes to see a circus in town. He describes his wonder and his enjoyment of the circus acts. He then returns to the show being put on by the Duke and King. This show is a failure and attracts only twelve people. The Duke redraws the handbills, advertising a spectacular show, 'The Royal Nonesuch', only for men.

COMMENT

Again Twain uses the device of placing contrasts next to each other to achieve his purpose. There are a number of 'shows' presented here.

Sherburn uses the words 'brave', 'bravery', 'manhood' to attack Southern ideas of chivalry.

Sherburn's bitter speech challenges the men in the crowd, accusing them of cowardice because of the actions that they are prepared to carry out as a crowd, but not individually. The speech appears exceptionally harsh, and it is undoubtedly Mark Twain making his own comments about men he has known.

By contrast the circus revives the wonder of childhood. Each of the acts is described vividly and with great enjoyment.

Compare Sherburn's speech with the description of the circus (see Language & Style).

Huck's visit to the circus provides a pleasant interlude. The climax of the show is a circus performer pretending to be a member of the audience and trying to get into the ring to ride horses. Huck's child-like absorption in what is happening is touching, 'It warn't funny to me, though; I was all of a tremble to see his danger' (p. 197).

Huck's innocent amazement when he realises the man is part of the circus act, should be seen in contrast to the description of the failure of the Shakespearean show of the King and Duke. The two men are not interested in entertainment but in money. The glorious and vivid representation of the circus is wedged between the two cynical presentations, of Sherburn and of the frauds.

GLOSSARY   camelopard an old word meaning a giraffe

CHAPTER 23

The revised show that evening is much more successful. The King painted as a tiger capers around the stage to great amusement.

'All I says is, kings is kings, and you got to make allowances' (p. 205).

The audience are angry that this constitutes the entire show, but agree to praise the performance so that they will not appear to have been fooled. The second night passes in a similar way, but the third night sees the townspeople intending to take their revenge. However, the Duke has anticipated this, and they escape. The group once again set sail down the river. Huck tells Jim about various kings, but mixes them up. Next morning Jim is homesick, thinking about his wife and children.

COMMENT   The behaviour of the King and Duke at the start of this chapter provides further evidence of the gullibility of Southern people, who allow themselves to be duped.

The discussion by Jim and Huck upon the nature of kings reveals Huck's limited understanding of the history which he has been taught, but also allows further demonstration of his lively wit and humour. It is an enjoyable episode which reinforces Jim's simple nature and his complete trust in Huck.

Notice the growing closeness of Huck and Jim.

A **motif** (see Literary Terms) running through the novel is Huck's continued awareness that his explanation of complicated ideas to someone with Jim's child-like understanding is impossible: 'What was the use to tell Jim these warn't real kings and dukes?' (p. 205). The deeply emotional story which Jim tells in his own dialect towards the end of this chapter, contrasts with the humour of Huck's tale, and also goes a long way towards establishing Jim as a true human being, a fact which Huck finds it difficult to accept. The chapter ends with Jim's words, uninterrupted by Huck, which offer a powerful comment on racism.

GLOSSARY   **shines** silly capers

Domesday Book commissioned in 1068 by William, King of England, a survey of all the lands in England, their value and ownership

Boston Harbour the Boston Tea Party, an incident in 1773 which led up to the American War of Independence

ornery here meaning more cruel, mean, than ordinary

CHAPTER 24

Coming to a village further down the river, the King hears about the death of a local man, Peter Wilks, whose brothers from England are expected. He learns that the brothers are a dissenting minister, Harvey, and William, a deaf and dumb man, and that they will be visiting their three nieces. Wilks was a substantial landowner and left a large amount of cash. The King dispatches Huck to bring back the Duke intending that they should pose as the brothers and steal the money.

COMMENT
It was enough to make a body ashamed of the human race (p. 215).

This is the beginning of the major act of deception practised by the King and Duke in the novel. In the following chapters their activities outrage Huck's fundamental honesty, forcing him to act to prevent the theft.

GLOSSARY   **dissentering** dissenting, a description of a minister belonging to other than the established religion in England

CHAPTERS 25–27

Having met the three nieces, Mary Jane, Susan and Joanna, the two frauds are told that $6000 inheritance money is hidden in the cellar. When they count the money it does not total that amount, so they supplement it from their own funds in case they should be suspected of theft. To allay further suspicion they make a gift of the full $6000 to the girls.

Observe Huck's growing concern, displaying his honest character.

The doctor, a close family friend of Peter Wilks, disputes the identity of the two men. The girls defend them and return the money to them to invest it on their behalf.

Huck is closely questioned by Joanna about his background and life in England. He is trapped in a number of lies but is rescued by Mary Jane, who defends Huck so completely that he decides to prevent the theft of their inheritance for her sake.

Consider why even though Huck steals, and tells lies, he is still seen as honest.

He steals the money from the King and Duke, and overhears their plans to sell the property, take the money from the sale, and escape. Huck hides the gold in Peter Wilks's coffin, intending to retrieve it later. However, people arrive for the funeral and the coffin is buried.

The following day, declaring their intention to take the girls back to England with them, the frauds sell the slaves. They discover that the gold is missing and when they question Huck he tells them that he saw the slaves behaving suspiciously.

COMMENT   Huck distances himself from the King and Duke, and his disgust at their behaviour in taking advantage of the goodness and innocence of the girls fuels his determination to foil their plans. He intervenes directly in this chapter, something he has never done before.

Enjoy the description of the funeral and the undertaker.   The description of the funeral, and of the undertaker in particular is highly comic as a caricature. Huck's description of him as 'softest, glidingest, stealthiest' (p. 239) provides a strong visual image which is sustained through the whole scene.

GLOSSARY   *Chapter 25*
doxolojer mispronunciation of doxology, a church hymn

Chapter 26
pallet a rough mattress
valley valet (mispronounced), a manservant to a person of significance

Fourth of July celebrated in the USA as Independence Day. It marks the signing of the Declaration of Independence in 1776 asserting independence from Britain

CHAPTERS 28–29

On the day following the funeral Huck tells Mary Jane the truth while trying to protect Jim from discovery. He informs her that the frauds are going to auction her property and then abscond with the money. He also tells her that the gold is hidden safely, but he is reluctant to tell her that the gold is in the coffin. He therefore writes down the details for her to find the gold later.

A question of identification.

Following the auction two men arrive claiming to be the real brothers, and an amusing scene follows. Both sets of characters attempt to prove their identity by claiming knowledge of what is tattooed on Peter Wilks's chest. When this proves inconclusive, the whole town goes off to the graveyard to exhume the corpse. They unscrew the coffin and find the bag of gold, and in the excitement Huck escapes. He reaches a relieved Jim on the raft and they set off quickly down the river. A short-lived feeling of freedom is brought to a close as Huck sees the King and Duke following them down the river, and they have to stop and pick them up.

COMMENT

Huck moves away from being an impassive observer and takes a direct hand here.

How is Huck's character confirmed in the episode with the Wilks family?

What we know of his intrinsic personality is enhanced and confirmed here: his quick-witted approach to stealing and hiding the money, and then using the mêlée to escape from the King and the Duke: his honesty of purpose in defending the innocent girls against the frauds: his disgust with Southern chivalry which proclaims it will defend the defenceless and weak but is powerless against true tricksters.

This is a more sensitive Huck than before.

The end of the chapter, when he has failed to escape the King and Duke, finds him almost unable to stop himself from crying.

GLOSSARY

Chapter 28
pluribus-unum literally means 'out of many, one' (formerly the United States motto *E pluribus unum,* here used satirically)

Chapter 29
chuckleheads fools

CHAPTER 30

The King and the Duke argue in the bitterness of having lost all their money. They blame Huck and Jim for having left them ashore, and each other for attempting to steal the bag of gold and hiding it. The Duke forces the King to admit that he hid the gold and on that note they retire to bed to become drunk and to reassert their comradeship.

COMMENT

The mutual distrust of the two frauds reveals the irony of their chosen identities. In their greed and anger towards each other there is nothing of nobility.

GLOSSARY

cravats scarves, neckcloths. Here used ironically to refer to the hangman's noose

CHAPTER 31

They drift south on the raft for a number of days until the two frauds feel safe enough to try to make money in various ways in the local villages, but they fail.

They spend some time discussing together the next plot, without involving Huck or Jim, and out of their

EXPLOITATION BY THE KING AND THE DUKE

Notice the change of hearing. Huck is uneasy. When he is ashore with the
tone. Huck and Jim two men, Huck decides to take the opportunity to
are separated from escape finally. He returns to the raft to find Jim gone.
the King and Duke He has been sold for forty dollars as a runaway slave.
and grouped Huck searches for him and tracks him to a farm owned
together. by Silas Phelps.

Huck's decision – Huck faces his conscience and debates what he should
for or against Jim? do. First he writes to Miss Watson, but he is still
unhappy. He tears up the letter and decides to rescue
Jim.

C OMMENT   Twain provides us with a crisis for Huck's 'sound heart'
in this chapter. Huck is angry and feels guilty at how
What do you think the frauds have treated them both. He finally comes to
about Huck's understand fully that Jim is not just a runaway slave,
reasons for his but a friend. Huck remembers the journey down the
decision? river, and Jim's gentle and loyal friendship, his many
kindnesses, and trust in him, and this prompts his
conscience: 'I'd got to decide, for ever, betwixt two
things, and I knowed it' (p. 283).

The choice he makes is for Jim and not the law, and he
tears up the letter to Miss Watson. He finally washes
his hands of the King and Duke and their problems,
'I'd seen all I wanted to of them, and wanted to get
entirely shut of them' (p. 288).

GLOSSARY   **doggery** a back street drinking house

A *Identify the speaker.*

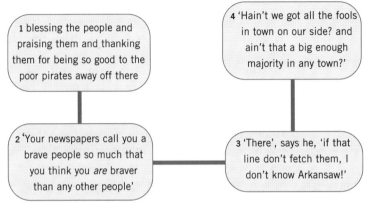

1 blessing the people and praising them and thanking them for being so good to the poor pirates away off there

4 'Hain't we got all the fools in town on our side? and ain't that a big enough majority in any town?'

2 'Your newspapers call you a brave people so much that you think you *are* braver than any other people'

3 'There', says he, 'if that line don't fetch them, I don't know Arkansaw!'

Identify the person 'to whom' this comment refers.

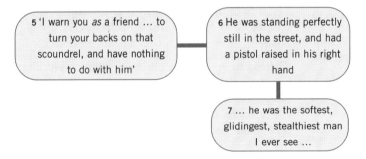

5 'I warn you *as* a friend ... to turn your backs on that scoundrel, and have nothing to do with him'

6 He was standing perfectly still in the street, and had a pistol raised in his right hand

7 ... he was the softest, glidingest, stealthiest man I ever see ...

Check your answers on page 95.

 B *Consider these issues.*

a Huck's changing attitude to the King and the Duke, where the change begins, and how you see it.

b Social customs, and how people are deceived by language.

c Huck's continually challenged conscience with regard to Jim.

CHAPTERS 32–43: JIM'S 'ESCAPE' AND HUCK'S FUTURE

CHAPTER 32

Huck arrives at the Phelpses' farm. He meets the woman he comes to know as Aunt Sally. She is expecting her nephew Tom Sawyer for a visit and thinks that Huck is Tom. When Huck realises this he is pleased as he knows Tom well, and can easily disguise his identity with stories about Tom and his family. The chapter ends with Huck realising that Tom will be actually arriving shortly and setting off, on the excuse of collecting his luggage, to meet him on the way.

COMMENT

This chapter returns to Twain's declared intention of writing a kindred book to *The Adventures of Tom Sawyer*.

What do you notice about the way the story is written in these following chapters?

The tone of the original story is re-established with the opening description of the farm which is recognisably a Southern farm. It brings back Huck's previous life.

There is an irony in the difference between Huck's real reason for being at the farm, i.e. to rescue his negro friend, and the reason for his delayed arrival given as the explosion of a cylinder head on the steamship which only killed 'a nigger' . It is clear that Twain was trying to re-establish a Southern folk-style story which, some think, does not sit very comfortably with Huck's previous struggles with his conscience.

GLOSSARY   **Baton Rouge** a town in the Southern state of Louisiana
                mortification infection of gangrene

CHAPTER 33

Huck meets Tom, who is surprised to see Huck, having thought he was dead. Huck explains why he is there, and Tom agrees to help rescue Jim. Tom arrives at the farm and announces himself as his brother Sid Sawyer.

With the arrival of Tom, notice the return to the boys' early relationship and change of tone.

At dinner, the boys try to find out about Jim, but without success. They do realise, however, that the King and Duke have been found out as frauds and that the local townspeople intend to tar and feather them that night. Huck and Tom try to get to town to warn them, but arrive too late. Huck describes the men as looking like 'a couple of monstrous big soldier-plumes' (p. 305).

COMMENT

Huck's sensitivity to another's plight is shown here.

'Human beings can be dreadful cruel to one another' (p. 305).

Despite the trickery of the King and Duke and that they have received their just deserts, he feels sympathy for them as human beings. He is a boy whose conscience plays a great part in his behaviour. 'It don't make no difference whether you do right or wrong, a person's conscience ain't got no sense, and just goes for him *anyway*' (p. 305).

Look back to the opening chapters where Tom and Huck play robbers. Identify the differences.

The contrast between the characters of Huck and Tom is re-established during the planning of Jim's rescue, with Tom taking the lead in inventing a fine adventurous escapade and deciding how it will be done. In many comments throughout the novel Huck refers to Tom as the daring one, noting how he thought Tom might behave, what he would do and think.

Huck professes himself to be astonished at Tom's willing participation in 'nigger stealing' (p. 299): perhaps a further attempt by Twain to restore the sense of adventure, and to put Huck's problems of conscience behind him. Certainly the following chapters seem to lose sight of the serious nature of the previous debate, by creating highly comic escapades.

CHAPTER 34

The two boys discover where Jim is being kept prisoner and each thinks of a plan for rescue. Huck's plan is simple but would probably be effective. Tom favours a more complex and detailed plan, which is more adventurous. They examine the area where Jim is being held, and Tom declares that they will dig him out. They see Jim during the daytime and tell him that they are going to rescue him.

COMMENT

Now begins a series of chapters which have been described variously as either ludicrous, or fitting for this story. Not only do the boys intend the rescue, but, at Tom's insistence, they plan to carry it out in as complex a way as he can think of.

Huck is the practical one, seeing the quickest and most effective way to achieve his goal, and Tom is the **Romantic** (see Literary Terms), drawn by his imagination and the fiction he has read into a world of fantasy.

'Here was a boy that was respectable … [making] himself a shame and his family a shame' (p. 308).

The slavery debate does reappear here, and may be seen as providing a link between the adventurous escape plan, and the seriousness of Huck's internal struggle. The story has not yet become a boys' escapade. Huck cannot understand why Tom will take part in rescuing a slave, and his conscience dictates that he says so. Later in the novel we learn that Tom knew Jim was free and had been so since the death of Miss Watson. The rescue is not the matter of conscience for him that it is for Huck. The reader here understands that Huck's character is given greater depth than Tom's, as he was prepared to sacrifice his soul and conscience to effect the rescue, while believing Jim a slave still.

GLOSSARY

bullinesses first-rate ideas deliberately introduced into the escape plan to keep it complicated

CHAPTERS 35–39

Notice how Tom adds new ideas to the plan. Do you find it amusing or absurd?

The plotting grows more complicated as Tom becomes more engrossed in it. Tom decides that Jim must be dug out, but using only knives as a prisoner would have no spade; he maintains that a rope ladder must be made out of sheets, even though Jim's hut is on ground level. He responds to Huck's objections by challenging his sense of adventure.

They decide to bake a 'witch pie' , a dish containing a rope ladder with a crust on top to hide it, which they plan to smuggle in to Jim. There are amusing scenes with the family as a sheet and other household items disappear because Tom has decided he needs them.

The final stages of the escape plan are entirely comic, and Tom wants to provide Jim with a grindstone to scratch his invented coat of arms and a message on, but needs both Jim and Huck to get it into the hut. Jim is

helped out of the hut in order to wheel it in, and is then restored to 'captivity'. The collection of a motley array of spiders and snakes to share Jim's cabin, despite

Jim's protests, sees Tom pronouncing them almost
ready to effect the rescue. The final touch is to send
anonymous letters to the Phelpses threatening an
attempted escape and warning of dire consequences for
anyone who gets in the way.

COMMENT   Tom is fully conversant with **Romantic** (see Literary
Terms) fiction from his own reading and makes full use
of it for the plan. The specific details of the plan in
these chapters are amusing, often highly comic as Tom
moves increasingly into the realms of the fantastic and
highly improbable.

Does Tom   Tom's increasingly fantastic plan, and the escapades the
successfully restore   boys indulge in are the focus of criticism of the final
the sense of   chapters of Twain's story. He allows Tom his head,
adventure?   despite Jim's increasing frustration and Huck's grudging
acceptance. Tom's reassurance of Jim that he should
not be afraid, '... because we would see that he got
away, *sure*' (p. 327) encourages the reader to enjoy the
escape plans as Jim will be rescued eventually.

GLOSSARY   *Chapter 35*
Trenck, Casanova, Chelleeny (Cellini) adventurers who all
managed to escape from prison, and who are associated with
the **Romantic** tradition
Iron Mask, Castle Deef the Man in the Iron Mask was a
mysterious state prisoner in the reign of Louis XIV of France;
Château d'If is where the hero of Alexander Dumas's novel *The
Count of Monte Cristo* is imprisoned

Chapter 36
counterpin counterpane, coverlet for a bed

Chapter 37
Mayflower name of the ship that in 1620 brought the Pilgrim
Fathers, emigrants from England to New England, where they
founded a colony

Chapter 38
scutcheon, dexter, etc. heraldic terms used wrongly by Tom, who is more concerned with the names than with the accuracy of their usage

Chapter 39
Tooleries Tuileries, part of the royal palace in Paris

CHAPTER 40

Having been alerted by the anonymous letters, there are fifteen armed men at the house the night of the escape. The boys finally rescue Jim, escaping just as the men approach the hut. They are seen and chased as far as the river where they sail in their hidden canoe to the raft. They are pleased that they have managed the escape, with Tom even more delighted that he has been shot in the leg. Huck realises that, despite Tom's protests, he must find a doctor. He sets off back to the village, leaving Jim hiding in the woods to watch over Tom.

COMMENT The adventurous escape is entirely pleasing to Tom, especially when he is shot.

'I knowed he was white inside' (p. 362). This turn of events produces the generous response in Jim that he will wait until Tom is tended by a doctor before going on, even though his freedom is still at risk. Huck is proud of Jim, but attributes his humanity to Jim's white soul, rather than his black skin.

GLOSSARY   **mosey** hurry
              Injun File single file

CHAPTER 41

The doctor arrives but, suspicious of Huck's explanation, declares that he will go out to the raft alone. Huck settles down to wait for him but falls asleep. The next morning he returns to the Phelpses' farm and hears the farmers' wives discussing the escape. They cannot understand the number and type of items found in the hut, and come to the conclusion that spirits might have helped, especially as no trace has been found of the escapees. Aunt Sally begins to worry about 'Sid'. Uncle Silas searches for him but cannot find him. Aunt Sally sends Huck to bed and sits up all night waiting for 'Sid' to return.

COMMENT   The description of the items found in the hut after the escape thoroughly confuses the women, and their conclusion, being so far from the truth, stresses the comic absurdity of the escape. It also allows Twain to poke fun at Southern people who resort to belief in the supernatural rather than their own knowledge. At the same time Twain allows the goodness and gentility of Aunt Sally to be seen in this complex handling of plot.

Huck is torn between worry for the safety of his friends and kind feelings towards Aunt Sally, who is so obviously distressed at Tom being missing.

Think about the differences between Twain's presentation of Aunt Sally here, and some other Southern characters earlier.

He spends a restless night, anxious to go and search for Tom and Jim, but bound by his honour not to break his promise to Aunt Sally. There is a gentle, sadly evocative description of her 'old grey head … resting on her hand, and she was asleep' (p. 372) which ends the chapter. She has ' mothered me so good … I couldn't look her in the face' (p. 371). Huck determines never to hurt such a good soul as her again.

CHAPTER 42

Tom returns to the Phelps farm, delirious with fever but alive. Jim has been recaptured and is locked up. The doctor describes how Jim left his hiding place to help

URBAN OUTFITTERS

LASGOW 81842931
RCH NO. 81842931

SWITCH

5759642689727450
VALID FROM 01/02
EXP 0104   SWIPED

THANK YOU

AMOUNT   £110.00

SIGN BELOW

Georgina Bowell

PLEASE DEBIT MY ACCOUNT
14:49 22/04/02   :
AUTH CODE:9534
SN 03434474   TXN 8602

Tom, and demands that he is treated well. When Tom recovers consciousness he boasts to Aunt Sally about the escape and the preparations for it. He declares that Jim is truly free, released by Miss Watson when she died and that the whole escapade was just an adventure. Aunt Polly arrives, informs Aunt Sally of the true identity of the boys, and confirms Jim's freedom.

COMMENT   The accepted Southern prejudice is given expression again, with the men blaming Jim for attempting to run away and creating 'such a raft of trouble' (p. 374).

Notice the range of comments Twain makes about the people and their attitudes.

The reader feels the injustice of this as Jim could have escaped if he had left Tom alone with his injury. He placed the life and safety of a friend above personal considerations. The farmers can see and accept this goodness in Jim, and yet divorce it from his slave status. This is the final and definitive contrast between Huck and the South.

Twain does not allow the farmers the last word. He uses **cynicism** (see Literary Terms) to criticise their 'noble' intentions. They do not want to incur any cost in doing what is right. Huck says that Southern people are brought up short when there is a conflict between principle and money: '[those who want to hang a slave] is always the very ones that ain't the most anxious to pay for him when they've got their satisfaction out of him' (p. 374).

'I thought he had a good heart in him and was a good man' (p. 376).

The doctor speaks in Jim's defence as he needed his help with Tom. However, this does not affect the farmers' physical treatment of him.

Tom's revelation, confirmed by Aunt Polly, that Jim is indeed free, provides an ironic backdrop to these comments by the people. The reader's response to Tom's declaration that it was all an 'adventure' could be one of anger against the manipulation of a simple, kindly man such as Jim. Huck, however, is now able to rationalise Tom's involvement in the rescue.

All the complications of identity and plot are settled in this chapter. Tom's ebullient description of the adventure is in sharp contrast to Aunt Sally's realistic appraisal of the events. 'So it was *you* ... that's been making all this trouble ... and scared us all almost to death' (p. 379).

The whole of the escape plan and the rescue take the reader back to the adventure story begun at the start of the novel. Innocence and childhood are restored; Huck and Tom reduced to being scamps and behaving as boys would.

CHAPTER 'THE LAST'

Tom and Huck discuss the preceding two weeks. Tom reveals that he intended to take Jim up river in style, tell him that he was free, and restore him to his home.

The adults are grateful to Jim for helping Tom and, now he is free, make a fuss of him. He is given forty dollars by Tom as a reward for 'being prisoner for us so patient, and doing it up so good' (p. 384). Jim reminds Huck of his fortune-telling at the start of their journey when he foretold that he was going to be rich again one day. Tom prepares for the next adventure, suggesting that the three of them should go into the Territory among 'Injuns'. Jim reveals that old Finn was the dead man in the floating house at the start of the story (Chapter 9). Huck finishes his 'book' by telling us that he has had enough story telling and intends to do no more. Sadly, he concludes by saying that he will leave for a new adventure before the rest as 'Aunt Sally she's going to adopt me, and sivilize me, and I can't stand it. I been there before' (p. 386).

COMMENT   The completion of several ideas introduced at the beginning is seen in this epilogue to the story.

- Jim has come through all of the adventures unscathed and leaves the story now a free man and with enough wealth to satisfy him. The reader is happy about this, feeling that Jim is vindicated and his simple gentleness appreciated.

- Because Jim is no longer a slave, the problem of 'friendship' does not exist. Now the group can plan adventures together.

- Huck's discovery of the death of his father has no apparent effect on him, but the reader is conscious of Jim's sensitivity towards his friend in having carried this knowledge throughout all their adventures.

- Twain presents Huck as still isolated at the end of the story, as much as he was at the start, not dependent on any one person for affection or guidance, able to make up his own mind and remaining true to the personality we have seen and enjoyed. The reader understands exactly what Huck means when he rejects 'sivilisation' : it is not for the likes of him, if it means accepting social rules which his conscience disputes and having to surrender the freedom his character demands.

- The irony with which Twain closes his story is contained in the final paragraphs. The book is a deliberately contrived event, he tells us, speaking as Huck, rather than the spontaneous story-telling which it appeared to be all the way through: 'If I'd a knowed what a trouble it was to make a book I wouldn't a tackled it, and ain't agoing to no more' (p. 386).

The tone of this ending is pessimistic, and Huck's intention to set out for new adventures is less a search for adventure than a retreat from society, as the whole novel has been.

A Identify the speaker.

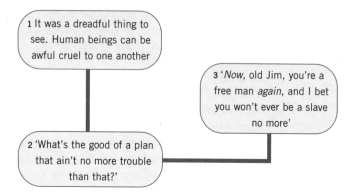

1 It was a dreadful thing to see. Human beings can be awful cruel to one another

3 '*Now*, old Jim, you're a free man *again*, and I bet you won't ever be a slave no more'

2 'What's the good of a plan that ain't no more trouble than that?'

Identify the person 'to whom' this comment refers.

4 I waked up at dawn ... and she was there yet ... and her old grey head was resting on her hand, and she was asleep

5 'He ain't a-comin' back no mo'

Check your answers on page 95.

B Consider these issues.

a Your response to the final chapters of this story: an adventure or a disappointment?

b Whether the ending is an optimistic or a pessimistic one.

c Whether Twain has drawn in Huck a character that you can admire and feel sympathy with.

d Whether the debate about slavery is sufficiently well presented for it to be taken seriously.

e How the structure of the novel was handled, in terms of comic and serious events, and how satisfactory was the ending.

Part three

Commentary

Themes

Themes are the main ideas which run as threads
through the text. It is possible to trace how themes are
developed by looking at:

- Individual characters and their interaction with each
  other
- Events and how they are portrayed

In this novel, because of the dominance of the major
character and narrator, Huck, all of the themes are seen
through him, his thoughts, actions, comments and
relationships. Principally we are asked to consider the
following:

- Freedom and restriction
- Integrity and hypocrisy
- Money
- Southern codes of behaviour

Freedom and restriction

Through Huck the restricted choices which individuals
face in living their own lives are shown. Huck and Jim
together symbolise the search for freedom in a number
of different areas:

- Physical freedom (seen both in Jim's attempts to
  escape from his life as a slave, and in Huck's turning
  his back on the Widow Douglas's and his father's
  ways of life)
- Cultural freedom (Huck's rejection of the restrictions
  of Southern society and his attempts to live
  without reference to Southern manners and
  customs)
- Mental and spiritual freedom (Huck's isolation from
  society. He is struggling to believe what his 'sound

heart' tells him, rather than accept the moral code imposed on him by the rules of society)

Physical freedom

The unifying element of the novel is Jim's escape from slavery. He is aided by Huck, as he tries to reach the free states.

The debate about slavery is the focus of the middle section of the novel. Look also at the discussion of mental and spiritual freedom below.

Jim' s physical journey down river provides a setting for a series of adventures, some serious and some comic.

Jim's journey ends happily when he discovers at the end of the novel that he has been freed on the death of his owner.

Huck's escape from his father and the Widow Douglas is also physically easy. He simply stages his death and moves away. Huck, however, is at the heart of a wider debate about freedom.

Cultural freedom

Huck's character is in conflict with the beliefs and customs of 'civilisation' as it is presented to him and to us throughout the novel.

Read the opening and closing chapters and try to decide what it is that Huck is resisting.

The novel begins with Huck railing against the Widow Douglas's attempts to 'sivilise' him, and ends with his decision to run away from Aunt Sally's attempts to repeat this process. In the course of the novel we observe Huck rejecting all of the Southern code of living (seen particularly in the restrictions imposed by regular schooling, religion and behaviour) in favour of the 'freedom' of life on the raft.

'Other places do seem so cramped up and smothery, but a raft don't' (p. 155).

There is nothing of the true **Romantic** (see Literary Terms) about this rejection; it is not an escape to a dream world, as life on the raft is shown to be dangerous and harsh in many ways. However, Huck's positive response to the river itself is more in keeping with his simple personality. He dislikes rules, and rejects formal religion with its beliefs which he cannot fully understand.

This is very much a reflection of the views of the writer. Twain is remembering his own life as a boy when he felt that one could be truly free. This was especially true of the time when he was working as a steamboat pilot on the Mississippi River (see Mark Twain's Background in the Introduction).

On the river Huck meets many different characters, all in their way examples of the Southern code of behaviour with which Twain was becoming dissatisfied. In contrast to how these people are seen to act and think, Huck's decision to remain true to his own principles and to reject those of society, is increasingly admired. However, the more he turns away from the people he meets, the more isolated he becomes.

Mental and spiritual freedom

In Huck we are shown a character who refuses to accept unquestioningly what other people believe. From the opening of the novel he attempts to look honestly at 'truth' in all of its forms.

Look in the early chapters for Huck's responses to prayer, heaven and hell.

He considers 'religion', and rejects the recognised format of prayer, heaven and hell in favour of his own understanding of what is acceptable and what is not. Twain early establishes a character who will decide for himself, and we carry forward this understanding of Huck's character into the central section of the novel, where he explores his motives for helping Jim escape slavery, and discusses the conflict between his conscience and civilisation: between what is right legally and what he feels is morally right.

Search for evidence of Huck's opinions about the societies he sees.

Twain allows us to witness this debate from its beginning. It arises simply as a refusal to allow Jim to be arrested for a murder he has not committed, and ends when Huck decides that he will go to hell rather than turn in his friend, Jim. He chooses the freedom to be able to respond to what he knows is right, and the reader agrees. However, this individual response isolates

Huck further from the South. At the end of the novel
Huck is no more free than he was at the start. He still
has to resist 'sivilising' although, the reader feels, with
more resignation and less enthusiasm than at the
beginning of the novel.

The end of his journey sees Huck virtually alone,
with no home, no family and no future, even with
'friends'.

INTEGRITY AND HONESTY

This area overlaps with the previous theme of freedom.
Huck is a simple and honest character, with a simple,
superstitious but respectful attitude to life, which
demands that he considers seriously all of the attitudes
and ideas he comes into contact with.

His character is a medium for Twain to present the
many dishonesties in the people and ideas Huck meets
on his 'journey' through Southern societies.

Religion
Religion is presented as part of a misunderstood belief
system.
- Miss Watson induces Huck to believe in 'spiritual
  gifts' (p. 14), and requires that he pays lip service to a
  belief in heaven and hell which he does not
  understand fully: 'I reckoned I wouldn't worry about
  it any more, but just let it go' (p. 15).
- The Grangerfords are a feuding family, bent on
  killing every member of the neighbouring
  Shepherdson clan, but unable to see the irony in their
  praise of a church sermon 'all about brotherly love'
  (p. 146).
- The camp meeting (Chapter 20) is a cynical
  demonstration of how simple a matter it is to defraud
  people who wish to show their belief in the principles
  of 'love thy neighbour' by contributing to a 'pirate

mission', but who are not able to distinguish the false from the true: 'come, pore and needy, sunk in shame! (*a-a-men!*) come all that's worn, and soiled, and suffering!' (p. 174). These words are enough to provoke undeserved support, without any further need to question the speaker.

Disguise

Huck invents a number of different stories about himself, in some cases to avoid identification, but also from a natural aversion to telling the whole 'truth' to people he barely trusts.

Note his astute awareness of character despite the humour of his tales.

In particular, he invents a story to explain to the King and Duke why Jim and he are travelling down river. In this case his caution is well-founded, but he is still unable to protect Jim from the King and Duke's money-grabbing schemes, or prevent them from selling him to Mr Phelps.

The humour which accompanies Huck's disguises helps the reader to accept that there is an essential difference between Huck's fabrications, and those of more ruthless individuals.

Fraud and exploitation

The King and Duke are important characters for a large part of the journey down river. Their effect on the harmony of life on the raft is immediately felt by Huck, and the reader watches their increasingly cruel exploitation of the river folk they meet.

How much of what they do is humorous and how much is unsettling to you?

Their behaviour angers and disgusts Huck, particularly when they plan to steal the whole inheritance of the three Wilks nieces. Huck declares himself to be so 'ashamed' by this stage that he intervenes directly to protect the girls from exploitation.

There is no morality in the behaviour of the King and Duke. They see no difference between the selling of Jim and any other of their money-making schemes. They have no conscience.

Conscience and integrity	The crisis of Huck's 'sound heart' as opposed to his cultural obligation is fundamental to the presentation of this theme.
Is Twain successful in presenting the importance of Huck's argument with his conscience about slavery?	Huck debates with himself by what moral authority he can refuse to return Jim to his owner, and there are points of tension where he comes near to handing Jim over to the authorities; however, each time he resists and it becomes harder for him to forget the human friendship the two of them have shared and to return to a one-dimensional view of Jim as a black slave.
Consider Jim's story about his daughter's deafness (pp. 206–7).	An important part of this debate is that Huck has begun to see that Jim has human feelings and emotions, simple for us to see, but difficult in the climate of Southern prejudice presented by Twain.
Is this ending too simple? Does it spoil the story for you? Would you prefer Huck to have to battle on against his society?	You may consider that this conflict was satisfactorily resolved, however, because Huck tears up the letter to Miss Watson and makes a firm decision to rescue Jim.
	But the story ends simply too. Jim is given his freedom and Huck does not have to go on justifying his actions.
Language and truth	Huck and Jim and their relationships with each other are open and honest, a fact which is reflected in their plain direct language. This is in direct opposition to the showy **rhetoric** (see Literary Terms) popular in the South. This Southern weakness is fully exploited by the King and the Duke.
	Perhaps the most direct statement as regards the theme of Integrity and Honesty should be left to the narrator, Huck, as Twain's mouthpiece. The opening paragraph of the novel begins with a statement about truth being only 'mostly' told by Twain in the previous novel, but 'with some stretchers' (p. 1). The end of the novel is signed 'yours truly' by Huck (p. 386) as an indication

that the novel is an attempt to give a true account of what is seen and understood by the main character, Huck.

MONEY

Although not directly a major concern of the novel, money does recur as a **motif** (see Literary Terms) on several occasions:

- Huck feels that to live on a dollar a day is 'more than a body could tell what to do with' (p. 1).
- Huck is valuable to his father because he has $6000 and so old Finn returns to claim his rights: 'The law takes a man worth six thousand dollars and upards, and jams him in to an old trap of a cabin like this' (p. 35).
- Jim is to be sold for $800 by Miss Watson, the threat of which induces him to run away.
- Jim tells the story of how he was rich once, and hopes to be so again (p. 61), a situation realised at the end of the novel when he is given forty dollars by Tom!
- Mrs Judith Loftus sees smoke on Jackson's Island and intends to search for Jim to claim the reward money.
- Two twenty dollar pieces are given to Huck by the slave catchers, so that he will sail past their town (pp. 120–1).
- The King and Duke work their tricks for money, including defrauding religious gatherings and putting on shows.
- The King and Duke attempt steal the Wilks girls' inheritance.
- Jim is sold for forty dollars by the King and Duke.

These are all instances where specific amounts of money are mentioned in the plot, and all have a direct bearing on it.

However, there is a contrast between particular amounts of money and the *value* and *worth* of other things, such as freedom and honesty.

Think about the difference between monetary value and true worth.

Huck is a rich boy. It is not this that will make him happy. The King and Duke make large amounts of money from their tricks, but they are not happy either. Neither are the Grangerfords, a well-to-do gentle family.

Huck and Jim are easily satisfied by the simpler things in life, and the reader knows that money is not the solution to either of their struggles.

SOUTHERN CODES OF BEHAVIOUR

The simple plot that Twain has constructed means that Huck and Jim are able to observe a variety of people as they sail down the Mississippi. The two characters are drawn in contrast to the values and actions of those they meet, and are largely critical of what they see. Much of this criticism has already been discussed, but it is worth drawing specific reference to areas Twain wishes to highlight.

Consider the effect on you of the unquestioning acceptance of slavery by e.g. Aunt Sally and Mary Jane Wilks.

- The primary and continuous criticism levelled at the South is its acceptance of the right of one person to own another as his property, that is, slavery. Twain passes over the economic reasons for its existence and directs the reader's attention onto the moral concerns. The theme of slavery is given more attention because it is presented by a Southern boy, Huck, a child of his times, who in the course of his journey comes to recognise qualities in Jim which are not present in other, white, characters.
- In the towns that Huck visits he witnesses incidents of violence, murder, drunkenness, laziness and arrogant speech-making. These together increasingly create a picture of a morally deficient South. The

Grangerfords and their outdated code of honour add
to the feeling that what the two fugitives see is a
sordid, barbaric and poverty stricken lifestyle. There
is ignorance and cruelty behind the outward show
of Christian belief, seen in the Grangerford family
and also in the camp meeting where the King is
easily able to defraud the people with comforting
words.

The whole picture when thus examined is of a people
desperately hanging onto an outmoded code of
behaviour, unaware that they are 'dreaming' life away,
out of touch with reality and sincerity. The contrast
with Huck's and Jim's honest and forthright pleasure in
the simple things of life, their awareness of what is truly
valuable as opposed to surface show, is clearly drawn by
the author.

STRUCTURE

The organisation of a novel in terms of its particular
form, presentation, and the positioning of events and
ideas, is called its structure. This is a deliberate device
on the part of the author, to ensure that the main
purposes for writing the work are clearly communicated
to the reader.

NARRATIVE STRUCTURE

The novel *The Adventures of Huckleberry Finn* itself was
intended by Twain to portray life on the Mississippi
River in the 1830s, before the American Civil War,
when, he felt, life was much less restricted.

The seemingly simple and uncomplicated plot is given
an overall unity by its being an account of a journey,
physical and **metaphorical** (see Literary Terms), made

by the principal character, Huckleberry Finn, and his companion, Jim, a runaway slave, (down the river from St Petersburg (Hannibal, Missouri) to below Memphis). The purpose of the journey is to help Jim reach a place of freedom, where he will no longer be a slave.

This provides the two fugitives with opportunities for a variety of adventures along the way. The episodic nature of this plot is called **picaresque** (see Literary Terms). As the journey proceeds, the mood of the narrative alters, providing Twain, through Huck, with the opportunity to deliver some mocking **satire** (see Literary Terms) and a condemnation of Southern life (discussed in some detail above, see Introduction on Context & Setting).

The novel can be divided into three major sections:

Chapters 1–7: Huck's 'sivilised' life with the Widow Douglas, the constraints and conflicts in his life between what he has to accept and what he really feels, up to the time when he decides to stage his own death and escape from both his father and the widow. In the Detailed Summaries, this section is further subdivided into two: *Chapters 1–4*, Huck's genuine attempts to come to terms with the rules and expectations he experiences while living with the Widow Douglas and her sister Miss Watson, and *Chapters 5–7* where he is kidnapped by his drunken father. The reader ends this whole section knowing that Huck will find no easy solutions in either of his lives. After his meeting with Jim, the runaway slave, the journey for both refugees begins as they set off to sail to towards Cairo and secure Jim's freedom from slavery.

Chapters 8–31: the long journey down river begins. As the journey progresses the two characters meet a variety of different people who represent those who lived on the Mississippi in the 1830s and 1840s: scoundrels, ordinary people, the oldfashioned people living according to a past code, the lazy, the foolish and the victimised. Again, this section is subdivided in the Detailed Summaries. *Chapters 8–18* provide a powerful central section containing many spectacular descriptions of nature, and imaginative descriptions of people (see Language & Style). They also provide the focus for the exploration of Huck's 'sound heart' as opposed to his 'deformed conscience' with regard to slavery (see Themes). Much of Twain's love for the river and his knowledge derived from his work as a steamboat pilot can be found in this section. *Chapters 19–31* sound a more sombre note, with the advent of the tricksters, the King and the Duke. It is in these chapters that Huck's increasing disgust with the two frauds and with the people they so easily fool comes further into perspective. Twain's biting **satirical** (see Literary Terms) attitude to the South and its hypocrisy is given voice in this section. It is worth noting at this point that Twain began the writing of this novel immediately after finishing *The Adventures of Tom Sawyer*, and wrote the first 400 pages, usually taken as ending with Chapter 16, without any trouble at all. However, he then came to a full stop, and struggled to write the remainder over the next seven years.

Chapters 32–43: the closing section. This section contains a comic description of the escape of Jim from the Phelpses' farm, and also presents Huck's determination to escape once again from the threat of adoption by Aunt Sally, another attempt to 'sivilise' him. This section is the subject of severe critical disagreement: some critics argue that it restores the novel to its original intention of a 'kind of companion to Tom Sawyer' as Twain himself called it, a sequel, an adventure story in the same **genre** (see Literary Terms);

others argue that it renders facile the moral debate experienced by Huck in the previous section.

Consider your own response to this choice of ending to the novel.

The novel begins with Huck's railing against a civilised society which is beset with restrictive practices, and ends with him determining to 'escape' again into the wilds of the 'Territory'. This controlled beginning and ending provide a circular plot which ensures a structured unity.

This plot control creates a sense of completion. The reader is satisfied that the essential character that is Huck has not been compromised or substantially changed in any way. He remains the free spirit he was at the start, and society has been unable to force him into giving up his freedom. It is a sad ending, however. His companion of the journey, Jim, faces a brighter future, probably with the prospect of being reunited with his family. Huck remains the isolated and intensely lonely boy he was at the start, without even the father he had then. Twain's pessimism is clearly stated through the fate he leaves his major character to face. However, one could argue that the novel would have been unrealistic if a happy ending for Huck had been manufactured. The ending is fitting for Twain's novel.

CHARACTERS

Think about these points as you study the following characters.

We learn about characters through:
- Their own actions and behaviour
- The way they speak, and what they are concerned about
- How they view other people and incidents
- How other people view them and speak about them
- Their relationships with other characters in the text
- What the writer tells us directly

HUCKLEBERRY FINN

Brave,
resourceful
Caring,
good-hearted
Practical,
realistic
Self-reliant,
honest

Find scenes and
incidents in the
novel to justify
this list.

Huck is the narrator of the novel. He is a young boy, thirteen to fourteen years old, the outcast son of a drunken, shiftless father. At the start of the novel he is living with the Widow Douglas.

The character of Huck is directly drawn from a boy Twain knew, Tom Blenkenship, the son of a local drunk living in Hannibal, the real setting for the town of St Petersburg. The boy was remembered by the author as being ignorant, unwashed, independent and good-hearted, qualities with which Twain endows Huck.

There is little direct physical description of Huck, leaving us free to visualise him and also to be more concerned with his emotional and spiritual qualities, which are the essential Huck.

Huck is the main character of the novel, serving two literary purposes:

- *Firstly*, he is our guide down the Mississippi river, introducing us in realistic dialect and idiom to a multitude of different individuals. He provides us with a viewpoint from which to make sense of what we see. With him, we journey **symbolically** (see Literary Terms) through Southern life. He deliberately takes no active part in the events he witnesses during the novel, until he meets the Wilks girls (Chapters 25–9). He directly intervenes here to prevent the Duke and the King robbing the girls of their inheritance (see Themes).
- *Secondly*, as a character in his own right, Huck is an honest, unassuming boy whom we grow to admire and appreciate, despite, or because of, his human weaknesses. Because we admire him we can appreciate the central section of Twain's novel and the focus on the slavery debate.

Huck has two 'friends' within the novel: Tom Sawyer, whom he apparently admires and looks up to, and Jim, his fellow fugitive from civilisation. Huck joins in Tom's boyish searches for adventure, but he rejects Tom's **Romantic** (see Literary Terms) values, both at the start when the Band of Robbers attack a Sunday School picnic, and more fundamentally at the end when he is concerned to help Jim escape slavery. This rejection of Tom's imaginative life in favour of the practical and realistic life Huck himself prefers, also allows us to see him as a down-to-earth character, much older in his outlook than his years.

Consider your growing understanding of Huck's dilemma. Think about the problems he faces over his friendship with Jim.

Huck's friendship with Jim is central and seen as presenting the struggle between 'a sound heart and a deformed conscience' (see Themes, and also the Introduction on Context & Setting).

- The opening words of the novel introduce Huck as a witty and humorous commentator on society, his comic accounts of incidents adding to the attraction of the novel as a whole. He is struggling to live within the bounds of regulated society, caring about the widow and her sister and their efforts to educate him, but distinctly maintaining his own attitudes and ideas. He refutes organised religion with its emphasis on heaven, seeing it as a continuation of 'civilisation' and rules. He opts for the 'freedom' of 'the bad place' (Hell) so that he does not have to compromise on the things he loves.

TOM SAWYER

Romantic
Impractical and immature
Somewhat cruel in planning Jim's escape

Tom is Huck's friend, introduced in his own novel, the forerunner of this one, *The Adventures of Tom Sawyer.* Romantic, about the same age as Huck, but from a fundamentally different background, Tom has living relatives in Aunt Polly and Aunt Sally. He is a more respectable 'scamp' than Huck.

- Tom is an organiser with a dominant personality. He is admired by Huck for having ideas and plans for adventures. Tom is essentially an impractical reader of fiction. He complicates escapades with detailed plans, but is unable to see the difference between serious events and humorous ones.
- Huck's change of attitude as he becomes more familiar with the dream-like but essentially corrupt Southern society is not to be found in Tom, and the two boys are even more distanced at the end of the novel than they are at the beginning. At the start they are divided by their intrinsic view of life; at the end by Huck's increased maturity resulting from his adventures with the unscrupulous elements of the South.

JIM

Jim is a black slave, owned by Miss Watson at the start of the novel. On overhearing her intention to sell him he escapes and begins his search for freedom. In this he is similar to Huck, likewise a refugee from Southern society, but unlike Huck whose search is more about mental and spiritual freedom, Jim's search is a very dangerous one and one that directly breaks the social law.

Trusting and naive
Superstitious
Devoted to Huck as his friend

- Jim is shown to have very noble qualities. He is willing to forfeit his own freedom so that Tom can have the medical help he needs when he is shot (Chapter 40). This fundamentally contrasts with Tom's games, with his knowledge of Jim's freedom but refusal to tell.
- Jim effectively fathers Huck in the absence of his real father, knowing that Huck was orphaned when they discovered the body of the murdered man in the first wreck they saw. He waits for the right time to tell him (Chapter the Last).

- Jim is genuinely hurt at being made a fool of by Huck, after the river fog in which they lose each other (Chapter 16), and one of the lessons Huck learns is that he should not treat Jim with less respect because of his colour.
- Jim's simple homespun response to life, both in his superstitions and in his lack of intellectual subtlety, provides much of the gentle humour of the novel. But he is more than a comic picture – he is a human being searching for dignity to live life in freedom.
- Jim is not caricatured by Twain but endowed with stoicism and loyalty. This directly contrasts with his treatment by the 'civilised' white characters of the novel. To Huck's credit he comes to see Jim in his true light, as a friend, but is only finally free of an unquiet conscience for helping Jim escape, when he realises Jim is really free.
- The relationship between these two central characters allows the reader to come to understand them more fully, and also to debate with Huck the question of freedom (see Themes). The two survive in each other's company against a backdrop of danger and unscrupulous actions, but also of the peace of the river. They drift in harmony, only facing danger when the outside world threatens. They are comfortable with each other. The scenes on the raft, following the escape from the fog (Chapter 16) and the Grangerford incident (Chapter 19) are among some of the most moving in terms of affection and friendship within the novel.

THE KING AND THE DUKE

Are their frauds amusing or cruel? These two characters appear in Chapter 19, following a hasty escape from a fraud gone wrong. They are comic creations, used by Twain as a vehicle both for satire and for condemnation of the South. The King is an older

*Comic characters
used to satirise
the South*

man, giving the impression of ruthlessness; the Duke is presented as younger and outwardly more attractive.

- They are both ruthless, deciding without a qualm upon the most effective method of obtaining money from the people they meet. The fact that Huck knows not to trust them warns the reader almost at once to watch them closely.

- The balance between their absurdity in their Shakespearean rehearsals, and their cunning in cheating the gullible, for example in the Nonesuch shows, is finely drawn. While we can laugh at them, we are also aware of the stupidity of the Southern people who are taken in so fully. Twain allows the men to work their confidence tricks through a subtle use of oratory (see Language), and a flagrant manipulation of public sentiment. The camp meeting (Chapter 20) worked by the King is a masterly exposure of folly, with Twain showing no sympathy for the crowd which allows religious sentiment to be used for financial gain.

- No-one is safe from their frauds, from the simply ignorant who are mocked by Twain, to the gently needy as the Wilks girls. It is in this last fraudulent scheme that their true cruelty is revealed, and Huck decides to take a direct hand in foiling them.

- Their final act, the sale of Jim for forty dollars, destroys any lingering amusement the reader, and Huck, may have felt at their behaviour. Their lack of nobility, despite their assumed noble titles, and their cruelty are clearly depicted.

OLD FINN

*Dangerous
Selfish
Violent
Demanding*

The powerful visual description of Huck's father, presented at the start of Chapter 5, and his subsequent behaviour enlist our sympathy for Huck and his adventures.

Old Finn's character highlights Huck's need to be self-sufficient.

- Old Finn's grasping demand of his 'rights' and of Huck's fortune contrasts with Huck's simple contentment with living on a dollar a day. He is seen symbolically as haunting Huck: 'I judged the old man would turn up again by-and-by, though I wished he wouldn't' (p. 16) and so invites yet more sympathy for Huck.
- Huck is seen to enjoy his father's free, untrammelled lifestyle in the cabin for a while after being kidnapped, but old Finn's violence is an equal incentive, along with the threat of being adopted, for Huck to escape completely.
- The character of Huck's father serves to show us Huck's resourcefulness and his independence of action. Old Finn is used by Twain to emphasise Huck's total isolation and essential loneliness: Huck must care for himself.

MINOR CHARACTERS

Minor characters are useful devices for an author to:
- Move the plot forward
- Expand on a theme
- Give information about background events
- Provide an opportunity for the reader to learn more about major characters

Ask yourself which of these characters are drawn more fully by Twain, and thus fulfil a slightly more complex function than others.

The novel abounds with character names, of both individuals and families, male and female, young and old. Twain is presenting a wide range of representations of Southern life in the people whom Jim and Huck meet on their journey down the river. The more significant of them are listed here. As you read about them consider their part in the novel and the purpose they serve, with reference to the points above.

Judge Thatcher

Huck's trusted banker. He looks after and invests Huck's money, giving him a dollar a day to live on, and

	keeping record of the interest payments. He, with the Widow Douglas, attempts to gain custody of Huck to free him from his father's grasp.
Widow Douglas	The woman who gives Huck a home at the start of the novel, and who is attempting to 'sivilise' him. She is a kindly woman with strict beliefs and attitudes about behaviour. She tries, jointly with Judge Thatcher, to gain legal custody of Huck, but is unsuccessful. Huck is keen not to hurt her, would like her to be proud of him, but feels restricted by the life she imposes on him and the fact that he is not able to accept her beliefs.
Miss Watson	Sister to Widow Douglas, living with her and Huck. She is remembered for her attempts to teach Huck to spell, and also to instruct him about religion and prayer. She owns Jim and it is her intention to sell him that incites Jim to run away.
Jo Harper, Ben Rogers, Tommy Barnes	Three of the boys making up Tom Sawyer's Gang.
Mrs Judith Loftus (Chapter 11)	Lives by the river. She sees through Huck's disguise as a girl when he is trying to find out what is known about his 'death'. She tells him that her husband is intending to search Jackson's Island and thus is directly responsible for Huck and Jim setting out down the river.
Jim Turner, Bill, Jake Packard (Chapter 12)	Three robbers discovered by Huck and Jim on a wrecked steamboat. Bill and Jake are overheard planning to kill Turner for betraying them.
The Grangerfords (Chs 17–18)	A Southern 'gentle' family involved in a continuous feud with the neighbouring **Shepherdsons**. The family is criticised by Twain as being involved in a long-

standing and violent feud which the young son, **Buck**, does not understand and cannot explain. They represent gentility, hospitality and other accepted Southern virtues, and are mocked for their lack of artistic taste. They attend Sunday church, enjoying a sermon on 'brotherly love', but not applying the lesson to their own life (see Themes). Finally, almost the whole family is wiped out in a large-scale battle, an event which sickens Huck.

Boggs *(Chapter 21)*	A fifty-year-old harmless but regularly drunken character in Bricksville. He is regarded as a well-meaning fool, but when he continues to threaten to kill Colonel Sherburn and ignores the warning he is given, he is shot in cold blood by the Colonel.
Colonel Sherburn (Chapters 21–2)	A 'proud-looking man' , about fifty-five years old, and well dressed, who shoots Boggs. The crowd decides to attempt to lynch him, and when they challenge him, the Colonel delivers a biting satirical condemnation of Southern manhood and bravery.
The Wilks nieces, Mary Jane, Susan, Joanna (Chapters 24–9)	The female inheritors of the estate of Peter Wilks, recently deceased. They are aged nineteen, fifteen and fourteen respectively. They are duped by the King and Duke into giving up their money and allowing the frauds to sell their property. Mary Jane is depicted as a beautiful red-headed girl, kindly and trusting, and she appeals to Huck's chivalrous nature.
The Wilks brothers, William and Harvey (Chapter 29)	Impersonated by the King and Duke. The real Wilks brothers are English, William a deaf and dumb man, and Harvey a dissenting English minister. They arrive in time to prevent the frauds from taking the proceeds of the auction of their property.
Aunt Sally	Tom Sawyer's aunt, forty-five or fifty years old, grey-haired, yet vigorous, lively and garrulous. The King has sold Jim to her husband, Silas Phelps. She is the butt of

the trickery that Tom and Huck use to fix Jim's escape, providing comedy in her response to the theft of her sheets and spoons. She is not all foolish, however, and through Huck's eyes she is shown to be a kindly woman intending to 'mother' him, and worried by Tom's disappearance following Jim's escape. At the end of the novel she intends to adopt Huck, a fact that depresses him.

Silas Phelps   Aunt Sally's husband, the farmer to whom Jim was sold. He is an old gentleman, less dominant than Aunt Sally, but seen as a solid, reliable and hospitable farmer. He shares the Southern tradition in his attitude to Jim.

Aunt Polly   On her brief appearance in the novel she is described as
(Chapter 42)   looking 'sweet and contented as an angel' (p. 380). She is able to identify Huck and Tom to Aunt Sally, and to confirm Jim's freedom granted to him on the death of Miss Watson.

There are many other groups of characters and individuals who are not given such distinct identities as these, and who make brief appearances at different stages in the story:

- The dead body in the floating house (Chapter 9)
- The ferry-man asked by Huck to rescue the robbers from the wrecked steamboat (Chapter 13)
- The slave catchers on the river (Chapter 16)
- The crowds at the revivalist meeting, and witnessing the murder of Boggs in Bricksville (Chapters 20–1)
- The circus performers (Chapter 22)
- The undertaker (a wonderful visual picture of the type) (Chapter 27)
- The mourners at Wilks's funeral (Chapters 27–8) and others, also one-dimensional, whose function is largely to people the story and the river as Huck and Jim travel south.

There are specific features of the style of this novel which are important to its interpretation and understanding.

- The novel is told in a 'first person' narrative, by the major character himself, Huck.
- The novel is in the **picaresque** style (see Literary Terms, and also Structure).
- The novel uses Southern dialects and idiom as its language base.

Narrative style

What differences would there be if the story were told by an objective narrator, rather than by Huck himself?

A first person narrative presents the novel through one person's eyes, and thus directly affects the way the reader sees it. This can have a limiting effect on the breadth of vision the reader gains of what is happening; on the other hand it can also allow the reader to become absorbed with the narrator, and have a clear vision of how (s)he thinks and feels.

In this novel it is important that we become very close to the narrator, in order to enjoy the variety of events he presents to us, and also to experience his crises of conscience. It is fundamental to the purpose of the author.

Picaresque novel

The episodic nature of the novel, the largest part of it in the form of a journey, allows Twain to present many different facets of life and experience as Huck and Jim travel down the river (see Structure).

Idiom and dialect

The story within the novel is given to us by Huckleberry Finn, using his own personal language style, and reproducing faithfully those other dialects he comes into contact with. In the explanatory note at the start of the novel Twain draws the reader's attention to these dialects, clearly demanding that they be considered seriously as a faithful reproduction of the original, and therefore as attempting to bring **realism** (see Literary Terms) into the novel. The deliberate use of these specific dialects also places the novel in the category of a **regional novel** (see Literary Terms).

Huck's dialect and idiom

Huck's use of language confirms our impression of him as an honest and direct character. He is holding a conversation with the reader, addressing him/her directly from the starting word 'you'.

He is a simple boy, with simple attitudes, and his language reflects his uncomplicated response to the physical, cultural and spiritual life which is called 'civilisation'. For example, this is his reaction when Miss Watson tries to teach him about religion: 'She told me to pray every day, and whatever I asked for I would get it. But it warn't so. I tried it. Once I got a fish-line, but no hooks. It warn't any good to me without hooks ... No, says I to myself, there ain't nothing in it' (p. 14). This down to earth, practical but humorous approach to life sums up the character that *is* Huck.

His conversations with Jim reveal their identical superstitious views of life and their complete trust and faith in, and acceptance of the natural world.

Jim's speech and character

Jim's Missouri dialect appears uneducated and drawling. The missing consonants and the emphasised vowel sounds adequately display the lack of education of someone in Jim's position. However, Twain does not sneer at him. He gives him some powerful speeches within the novel, humorous as well, when he is discussing superstitions and fortune telling. Twain endows him with a nobility which is necessary to the overall message of the novel, and Huck, as well as the reader, is affected by his simple honest emotion. For example, following the river storm when Huck loses and then finds Jim, he pretends that he has been on the raft all of the time, and that Jim has dreamt the storm. Jim realises he is being fooled, 'my heart waz mos' broke bekase you wuz los', en I didn' k'yer no mo' what become er me en de raf' ... En all you wuz thinkin' 'bout wuz how you could make a fool uv ole Jim wid a lie' (p. 115). Language is used to emphasise this central relationship in the novel, and by the direct use of dialect the two characters are drawn ever more closely together.

FIGURATIVE LANGUAGE (see Literary Terms)

What particular language features do you notice most in the novel?

There are many thrilling moments in the novel which are rich in **imagery** (see Literary Terms). Twain, through Huck, presents passages of vivid description in a number of different contexts, some of which are given below as examples. Notice, however, that the whole of Huck's speech is full of descriptive imagery; these are not isolated examples:

- Descriptions of the sights and sounds of nature as Huck and Jim both live on the raft and sail the river
- Use of **simile** (see Literary Terms): 'everything still as rocks' (p. 54) to communicate loneliness, and the sky 'as bright as glory' describing lightning (p. 65).

Reread pp. 156–9. Pick out the references to sights and sounds.

- Use of **onomatopoeia** (see Literary Terms) to present sound images, 'a jingling of bells to stop the engines, a powwow of cussing, and whistling of steam' (p. 126)
- Use of **personification** (see Literary Terms) to suggest the range of noises, the 'lightning kept whimpering' (p. 97), the steamboat 'coughing' (p. 157)
- The description of the circus (pp. 195–7) with its long sentences, list-like, presenting colour and

energy, movement, and using a wide range of verbs and some literary devices such as:

hyperbole (see Literary Terms): dressed in clothes that cost millions of dollars, and just littered with diamonds' (p. 195)

- The description of the undertaker at the funeral of Peter Wilks, Chapter 27. It is a highly imaginative and comic description of the man: 'He was the softest, glidingest, stealthiest man I ever see' (p. 239).

Humour

Find further examples of the range of humorous devices listed here. Try to make the selection as wide as possible.

Because the language of the novel is peculiarly idiomatic, Huck's personal viewpoint provides an often humorous view of the events and people he contacts. Humour is also employed as a deliberate thematic tool by the author, and there are many instances of its use.

- Mockery, of the Southern people and their response to the murder of Boggs by Sherburn (Chapter 22, pp. 193–4)
- **Cynicism** (see Literary Terms) directed against such people as the Grangerfords who enjoy a sermon on brotherly love but see no message for themselves to follow (Chapter 18, p. 146)
- **Sarcasm** (see Literary Terms) used against the people at the camp meeting who are duped by the King's hollow words (Chapter 20, p. 174)
- Gentle amusement, as in the description of the undertaker (Chapter 27, pp. 239–40)
- The absurd, employed many times, particularly in the escape plans for Jim prepared by Tom and Huck (Chapters 35–40)
- **Malapropism** (see Literary Terms): Twain makes a character ridiculous through the manner of expression as well as the substance of what is said. Thus the King uses 'funeral orgies' or 'funeral obsequies' and refers to the dead man as 'the diseased' (p. 222)

PART FOUR

STUDY SKILLS

HOW TO USE QUOTATIONS

One of the secrets of success in writing essays is the way you use quotations. There are five basic principles:
- Put inverted commas at the beginning and end of the quotation
- Write the quotation exactly as it appears in the original
- Do not use a quotation that repeats what you have just written
- Use the quotation so that it fits into your sentence
- Keep the quotation as short as possible

Quotations should be used to develop the line of thought in your essays.

Your comment should not duplicate what is in your quotation. For example:

> Huck in his struggles to accept Jim as a person rather than a black slave, is surprised to realise that Jim cares the same about his family as white people do. He says, 'I do believe he cared just as much for his people as white folks does for ther'n' (p. 206).

Far more effective is to write:

> Huck in his struggle to accept Jim as a person rather than a black slave, is surprised to realise that Jim 'cared just as much for his people as white folks does for ther'n.'

The most sophisticated way:

> As Huck comes to accept Jim as a fellow human being, not just a slave, he realises that Jim cares as much for his family as 'white folks' (p. 206) care for theirs.

When you use quotations in this way, you are demonstrating the ability to use text as evidence to support your ideas – not simply including words from the original to prove you have read it.

Everyone writes differently. Work through the suggestions given here and adapt the advice to suit your own style and interests. This will improve your essay-writing skills and allow your personal voice to emerge.

The following points indicate in ascending order the skills of essay writing:

- Picking out one or two facts about the story and adding the odd detail
- Writing about the text by retelling the story
- Retelling the story and adding a quotation here and there
- Organising an answer which explains what is happening in the text and giving quotations to support what you write

- Writing in such a way as to show that you have thought about the intentions of the writer of the text and that you understand the techniques used
- Writing at some length, giving your viewpoint on the text and commenting by picking out details to support your views
- Looking at the text as a work of art, demonstrating clear critical judgement and explaining to the reader of your essay how the enjoyment of the text is assisted by literary devices, linguistic effects and psychological insights; showing how the text relates to the time when it was written

The dotted line above represents the division between lower and higher level grades. Higher-level performance begins when you start to consider your response as a reader of the text. The highest level is reached when you offer an enthusiastic personal response and show how this piece of literature is a product of its time.

Coursework
Essay

Set aside an hour or so at the start of your work to plan what you have to do.

- List all the points you feel are needed to cover the task. Collect page references of information and quotations that will support what you have to say. A helpful tool is the highlighter pen: this saves painstaking copying and enables you to target precisely what you want to use.
- Focus on what you consider to be the main points of the essay. Try to sum up your argument in a single sentence, which could be the closing sentence of your essay. Depending on the essay title, it could be a statement about a character: Jim, the black slave, is presented with dignity within the novel *The Adventures of Huckleberry Finn*, and shows himself to be the only true and loyal friend that Huck has; an opinion about setting: The Mississippi River is at the heart of the novel, providing not only the physical environment but also the representation of Southern life which so concerned Twain; or a judgement on a theme: The main concern of the novel *The Adventures of Huckleberry Finn* could be seen as that of freedom, physical and spiritual. Both Jim and Huck are attempting to escape from a civilisation which forces them into a lifestyle they do not want, and both are seeking a place where they can live according to their inner feelings rather than the laws of the land.
- Make a short essay plan. Use the first paragraph to introduce the argument you wish to make. In the following paragraphs develop this argument with details, examples and other possible points of view. Sum up your argument in the last paragraph. Check you have answered the question.
- Write the essay, remembering all the time the central point you are making.

- On completion, go back over what you have written to eliminate careless errors and improve expression. Read it aloud to yourself, or, if you are feeling more confident, to a relative or friend.

Examination essay

The essay written in an examination often carries more marks than the coursework essay even though it is written under considerable time pressure.

In the revision period build up notes on various aspects of the text you are using. Fortunately, in acquiring this set of York Notes on *The Adventures of Huckleberry Finn,* you have made a prudent beginning! York Notes are set out to give you vital information and help you to construct your personal overview of the text.

Make notes with appropriate quotations about the key issues of the set text. Go into the examination knowing your text and having a clear set of opinions about it.

In most English Literature examinations you can take in copies of your set books. This in an enormous advantage although it may lull you into a false sense of security. Beware! There is simply not enough time in an examination to read the book from scratch.

In the examination

- Read the question paper carefully and remind yourself what you have to do.
- Look at the questions on your set texts to select the one that most interests you and mentally work out the points you wish to stress.
- Remind yourself of the time available and how you are going to use it.
- Briefly map out a short plan in note form that will keep your writing on track and illustrate the key argument you want to make.
- Then set about writing it.
- When you have finished, check through to eliminate errors.

To summarise,   • **Know the text**
these are keys   • **Have a clear understanding of and opinions on the storyline,**
to success   **characters, setting, themes and writer's concerns**
                   • **Select the right material**
                   • **Plan and write a clear response, continually bearing the question**
                     in mind

Sample essay plan

The sample essay plan given here will show you how to structure an essay. It is divided into six parts, and the points are made in note form so that you can think them out for yourself. This is only one possible plan.

The relationship between Jim and Huck is important to the novel. Trace the growth of this relationship as the novel progresses, describing the main points in its growth.

Part 1:
Introduction

Huck and Jim are shown to know each other as they live in the same household at the start of the novel. Superstition is a link between them. Show that their relationship forms a large part of the theme of friendship in the novel.

Part 2:
How the two
become
fugitives

Huck, after having been kidnapped by his father, decides to stage his death and run away. Explain why Jim has run away and where they meet up. Explain here the difference between Huck's turning his back on civilisation, and searching for freedom culturally, and Jim's physical escape from being sold. Show the comfortable relationship they have, their shared experience as fugitives, and how this provides the basis for their river journey.

Part 3:
The way they
get to know
each other

Notice Huck's sense of adventure, his courage and his use of initiative. Huck has culturally limiting views of Jim as a 'nigger'. What does Huck do and say to reveal them? Notice also Jim's trust and reliance on Huck.

Remember here his discovery in the first wreck that Huck's father is dead, and also that he does not tell Huck until the end. What do such things show about Jim and his character?

Part 4:
Huck's
internal
conflict and
the crisis

Show how Huck becomes increasingly concerned about the moral rightness of his actions in helping Jim escape. What is the turning point for Huck? Explain why you have chosen this as an important point in their relationship. Contrast Huck's feelings with the behaviour and attitudes of other people seen in the novel.

Part 5:
The
relationship
under threat

Look at some of the changes which happen when the raft is shared by the King and the Duke. Notice how the episodic nature of the novel allows Jim to be left on the raft while Huck observes the range of people on shore. Show how Huck comes to his decision to help Jim escape from the Phelpses.

Part 6:
Conclusion

Bring in the discovery of Jim's true freedom from slavery and Huck's relief that he has not committed an unlawful act. Is his conscience quite clear that slaves should be freed, or is it a sign of the depth of his relationship with Jim that he helped him to freedom? Compare their circumstances at the end of the novel, with one free and the other yet again looking for an escape.

This is a basic plan which would cover most of the important aspects of the relationship. It is not necessary to explain every single event which could be used. Select the important parts and use them to discuss the essay title. You could improve the grade by:

- Using relevant selected quotations as support (see section on How to Use Quotations)
- Making it clear that you know the author is shaping the plot, themes and characters, that the novel is a created text with several purposes. You indicate this

by using such phrases as 'the author uses the character of Huck', 'the reader is asked to consider'

- Including comments about Southern society and about the Mississippi (see Introduction on Context & Setting)

- Including comments on the language styles chosen for the novel, the narration by Huck, and the use of dialect to encourage close identification with the characters

- Relating the content of the question to Twain's overall purposes, his growing disenchantment with Southern society and its defects

FURTHER QUESTIONS

The following questions are possible essay titles for examinations and coursework. Look back at the Essay Writing and How to use Quotations sections and then attempt the questions below.

1 Trace the growing relationship between Jim and Huck, describing the main events and points in its growth (see Sample Essay Plan).

2 How does the way that the story is told, with Huck as the narrator, affect the way that the reader sees the novel?

3 Would you describe the novel *The Adventures of Huckleberry Finn* as an optimistic or a pessimistic book? Consider the main theme, and also the ending, in your answer.

4 Explain how each of the three major characters of the novel, Huck, Tom and Jim, is important to our understanding of what the novel is about.

5 Consider the chapters which deal with the escape of Jim from the Phelps farm (Chapters 34–40). How do you respond to these chapters as a fitting ending to the novel as a whole?

6 How does the author present Southern society in this novel?

7 Imagine that you are asked to write about the character of Huck from the point of view of some of these people. Consider what you would say if speaking as:

    Jim   Aunt Sally
    Tom   The King and the Duke
    Widow Douglas

8 As Jim, write your account of your escape from Miss Watson and journey down the river. (Think about Jim's situation at the start and his slave status. You should select three to four major events to write about, from different parts of the text.) Try to give a realistic response to your life in the Southern states at this time.

9 Explain why *The Adventures of Huckleberry Finn* should be seen as more than a boys' adventure story.

10 For what different purposes does Twain use language within the novel and how effective is he in doing so?

11 Select four scenes which you think are vital to the overall success of the novel and explain your choice.

12 Imagine that at the end of the novel Huck is reviewing his actions in helping Jim to escape. Write two speeches which you could make to discuss what he has done:

    a In support of his friendship with Jim. Convince Huck that he was completely right to help Jim escape

    b Attacking Huck's actions in helping Jim to escape, based on the law and his duty to the state

Use specific sections from the text in your answer.

13 What reasons would you offer to students of your age as justification for studying this novel?

PART FIVE

CULTURAL CONNECTIONS

BROADER PERSPECTIVES

OTHER WORKS BY TWAIN HIMSELF

Think about what you want to read in an adventure story. Ask yourself if The Adventures of Huckleberry Finn *fits comfortably into this idea.*

- If *The Adventures of Huckleberry Finn* is your first Twain novel, try reading its predecessor *The Adventures of Tom Sawyer* and comparing the author's approach in that novel to the one you are studying.

  The Adventures of Tom Sawyer is more the boys' adventure story you expect. It introduces the main characters to the reader and has well-drawn moments of tension which truly make it an enjoyable work of fiction.

- Twain's *Life on the Mississippi* is not a work of fiction but a series of remembered incidents from true life, and is also an enjoyable read for the enthusiast, placing the importance of the river firmly in the reader's mind. The writer's love of the life he lived in early adulthood and its powerful influence on him are clearly expressed. It is also an interesting historical document of the times.

WIDER READING

There are several fictional works to enhance your understanding of the black *vs* white problems in the Southern states of America.

- The classic American slave novel *Uncle Tom's Cabin* (Harriet Beecher Stowe) establishes the prevalent attitudes to slaves at the time of Twain's novel. Although it is often regarded as exaggerated, and Southern people dispute its authenticity as a true account of events, it confirms Jim's fears about recapture, and supports Twain's assertions that Judith Loftus's husband was about to search for Jim using bloodhounds.

- *To Kill a Mockingbird* (Harper Lee) is a beautifully written portrayal of a white girl's growth in understanding about prejudice and its effects in the 1930s Southern states. Some of the general characters in *The Adventures of Huckleberry Finn* can be identified in this novel, in the white, privileged, but undeserving classes.
- *Roll of Thunder, Hear my Cry* (Mildred Taylor) is a powerful reconstruction of the life of black children, again told through the eyes of a child, but here a black child, in the Southern states. The novel clearly presents the attitude of white people to a black population released legally from slavery after the Civil War, but still suffering because of their black skin.

TEST ANSWERS

TEST YOURSELF (Chapters 1–4)
A 1 Tom Sawyer *(Chapter. 2)*
••• 2 Jim *(Chapter 4)*
3 Huck Finn *(Chapter 1)*
4 Huck Finn *(Chapter 1)*
5 Judge Thatcher *(Chapter 4)*
6 Huck Finn *(Chapter 2)*
7 Miss Watson *(Chapter 3)*

TEST YOURSELF (Chapters 5–7)
A 1 Old Finn *(Chapter 5)*
••• 2 Huck Finn *(Chapter 6)*
3 Old Finn *(Chapter 6)*
4 The Judge *(Chapter 5)*
5 Widow Douglas *(Chapter 6)*

TEST YOURSELF (Chapters 8–18)
A 1 Jim *(Chapter 8)*
••• 2 Huck Finn *(Chapter 8)*

3 Jim *(Chapter 15)*
4 Buck Grangerford *(Chapter 18)*
5 Huck Finn *(Chapter 16)*

TEST YOURSELF (Chapters 19–31)
A 1 The King *(Chapter 20)*
••• 2 Colonel Sherburn *(Chapter 22)*
3 The Duke *(Chapter 22)*
4 The King *(Chapter 26)*
5 The King *(Chapter 25)*
6 Colonel Sherburn *(Chapter 21)*
7 The undertaker *(Chapter 27)*

TEST YOURSELF (Chapters 32–43 The Last)
A 1 Huck Finn *(Chapter 33)*
••• 2 Tom Sawyer *(Chapter 34)*
3 Huck Finn *(Chapter 40)*
4 Aunt Sally *(Chapter 41)*
5 Old Finn *(Chapter 43)*

alliteration repetition of a consonant in words lying next to each other, so that an accumulated effect of the sound is created. Could be either a harsh, strident sound, e.g. 'it was just about the bluest and blackest – *fst*! it was as bright as glory' (p. 65) or a softer sound, e.g. '... nothing to see – just solid lonesomeness' (p. 157), depending on the letter being repeated

colloquialisms informal speech using everyday forms of words and grammar

cynicism a bitter reaction to a situation, custom or event, pointedly noticing the gap between what is said or done, and the reality

dialect a variety of speech belonging to a specific region or social background, with its own peculiarities of pronunciation and vocabulary

figurative language general term for the deliberate use of words to create an effect rather than simply to explain meaning

genre a specific form which literature takes, e.g. poetry, prose, drama, picaresque novel

hyperbole deliberate exaggeration for effect

idiom language of a particular form, related to characteristic speech patterns

imagery general term for descriptions which can be imagined, seen visually or absorbed through the senses

irony use (usually satirical) of words whose real meaning is only understood by a privileged audience

juxtaposition the placing of ideas next to each other to achieve a specific effect

malapropism wrong use of a word, with humorous effect. Named after Mrs Malaprop, a character in R.B. Sheridan's play, *The Rivals*, who constantly mixed up words. Here used by the King

metaphor a comparison in which it is stated that something 'is' another thing rather than that it resembles it

motif an idea or a theme which recurs throughout the text

onomatopoeia use of words which actually imitate the sound they describe, e.g. screech, bang

personification the endowing of inanimate objects with human characteristics

picaresque novel an episodic form of novel in which a sequence of events is described (often in the form of a journey), all aiming to create a picture of the whole

realism form of writing which attempts to describe things, events, situations as they really are

regional novel a novel which relies for its effect on being identified with a particular area, in geographical terms, and also in customs and speech

rhetoric language which is used to impress or persuade, and is often associated with insincerity

Romantic connected with a literary movement in England and Europe generally in 1770–1848. Following the revolutions in France and America, its main features were a concentration on elaborate themes inspired by nature, beauty, heroism and unrequited love, and a free and imaginative style

satire an attempt to ridicule a section of society or a person by pointing out some foolishness or absurdity, often cruelly. The intention is to stress the difference between what is and what should be

simile a comparison, stating that something is like, or comparable to, another thing

symbol a simple idea or object which is used to convey a more complicated idea